30 DAY SPENDING DETOX

The Simple Plan to Save Money and Get Out of Debt in One Month

---

TRACEY EDWARDS

traceywritesbooks

Disclaimer: This book contains information regarding general personal finance that is the author's own opinions and experiences. It is published for general reference and is not intended to be a substitute for independent verification by a professional financial planner or accountant. The publisher and author disclaim any personal liability, either directly or indirectly, for the information contained within. Although the author and publisher have made every effort to ensure the accuracy and completeness of the information contained within, we assume no responsibility for errors, inaccuracies, omissions, or inconsistencies.

 Created with Vellum

30 DAY SPENDING DETOX

Contents

Introduction

Could you go a whole month without spending?

Yes, you read that right, a whole month without spending any extra money. There will be things that you still have to pay for, like rent/mortgage, bills, and food, of course. I don't want you to starve, or live without shelter, or electricity.

But to stop spending on those other things that are not essential for survival. For one month.

Do you think you could do it?

I have a confession to make.

You would think that I would know better, considering I've written books on personal finance, but I'm embarrassed to admit that, over the past few months, our credit card bills have been getting higher and higher, and we have accumulated about $10,000 in credit card debt.

I know.

Now, I don't want to make excuses for why it happened (but it involved a crappy stock market, hubby being out of work, him breaking a collarbone, and me not being able to write because two small children don't exactly give you much time to yourself over the course of a few months), and I freaked out a little bit.

Okay, a lot.

You would also think that this would be enough of a reason to want to drastically change my spending habits and become more frugal during such a time.

I didn't. WE haven't (yes, family, I'm not taking the entire blame, here, this involves you, too).

Perhaps it was because we were all in denial, thinking that things would get better. The stock market would become positive again in time (and it will, it's just a waiting game, right now), hubby's shoulder would heal and he'd get back to work, the kids would grow up and I'd have more time to write.

But that's all in the future. It didn't help me right now. And right at that moment, we were not doing as well as we would have liked.

It wasn't until a few weeks later that I knew things had to change.

Baby Girl had a cold and was having trouble breathing through her nose, so I was frantically searching the house for the baby Vicks. The more I couldn't find it, the more frustrated I was getting, until I got to the point that I yelled to Husband that I'd had enough. We had too much stuff. I couldn't find anything. It wasn't the first time something had been lost inside the vortex of our home.

Now, I know what you are thinking: that I must live in a house like a hoarder's to lose so many things. Well, that's not true; I hate clutter, and do whatever I can to eliminate it. We live in a regular house, which is sometimes clean, sometimes untidy. It's a normal representation of how most people live, I would say. And, while my organizational skills could probably do with some work in keeping things where they should be, it was at that precise moment that I knew something was wrong. I had too much stuff.

That was where all our money was going. On stuff.

Something had to change. My solution was simple, if not a bit radical. I would just stop buying more stuff. Stop SPENDING.

Obviously, I had everything that I needed, already, hiding in the house somewhere, so I didn't need an extra moisturizer that promises a wrinkle-free forehead, or a new magazine showing me what my house could look like if I didn't have kids and a cat.

How much could I have saved in a month if I just stopped spending?

A lot? A little?

Obviously we would still have to spend some money - the kids get cranky when we don't give them dinner, and the electricity bill needed to be paid, because you can't watch Grey's Anatomy with no power. Still, there were so many little things that we buy without thinking: a can of Pepsi here, a lip gloss there. It all adds up.

But that wasn't all, no, this would also be a great time to get rid of some things I no longer used. I could even sell some of it on eBay, and make a few bucks. Books that I hadn't read in years, decorative items that I didn't even like, but just had on display because I had the space to put something there, and clothes that the kids had outgrown months ago.

It all had to go. I needed room to breathe. And I needed to reclaim my budget back. We needed to kick that credit card debt to the curb, where it belonged.

So, it was time to make myself a guinea pig, and see if I could go thirty days without spending money, and hopefully make a dent in paying back the credit cards.

Thirty Days.

Could I really do it?

The rules were simple: I could spend money on food from the grocery store and necessary toiletries. If an emergency came up, such as health, then I could spend money on those items/medicines that I needed.

I could not spend money on anything else. Nothing. Nada. Not even a cent.

For one whole month. Good god, what had I signed myself up for?

This challenge is not for the faint-hearted. It takes a lot of commitment to stop buying things, even if it's just for one month. We are all so conditioned to pop into the store to browse the aisles for something that takes our fancy, or buy something new when the old one fades and is no longer 'in fashion'.

Much of our spending is out of control, and, if it takes doing something extreme to open our eyes to see or learn a different way of doing things, even if it's just for the experience, then it's worth it.

By coming along on this journey, you'll find that it will change the way you view your spending, debt, and the need to accumulate.

There will be short term benefits, too, the most obvious being that you'll save a lot of money in a short period, which can help with your savings or for paying down debt. Plus, you'll have more free time. You might even find you like the peace of stepping out of the shopping hustle and bustle for awhile. Or, you might be craving to get back into the mall again after it's finished. Who can tell?

I can promise you that if you open up your mind and close your wallet, just for one month, not only will your bank balance look healthier, but you'll start to question if you really need what you are buying. You'll think differently about every purchase you make.

And, even if at the end of the thirty days it doesn't change you or your spending habits, at least you'll know that it was your choice, and you are in control. And gaining control of your spending, whether it changes you or not, is what this challenge is all about.

So, what do you say? Are you with me?

ONE

The Rules of the 30 Day Spending Detox

What exactly is a thirty-day spending detox? Is it some sort of crazy new diet where you only eat chocolate éclairs for a month? No, of course not (but if you do hear about that diet, please let me know).

Put simply, it's a plan to cut your costs dramatically within a month by not spending money on anything unnecessary.

It's not a new idea, and people have been doing no-spend months for years with great results. So, if you've ever thought of doing one yourself, this book will act as a guide on getting started, getting prepared, an explanation of the pitfalls you might encounter, and what to do after the month is over.

I won't lie to you. A money detox will be a radical change in your spending patterns, and it will be a challenge (but a fun one). It will also be a positive step toward leaner debt and a healthier financial future. And isn't that worth a small sacrifice now?

If you've been contemplating jump-starting a new spending and savings plan, then you know that it can be done one of two ways. You can either gradually make little changes along the way, or you can make a stand and dramatically shake things up.

Both can work, of course, but sometimes you just want to get things started immediately, detox your bad spending habits, and change your thinking about money. And you want it to happen fast.

That's what this plan is about: fast change, and dramatic results in just 30 days, or your money back (or something like that).

But it isn't just your money situation that will be better. Going cold turkey and not spending anything for a month can be empowering emotionally, because you'll know you can do it (because you just did).

It is great for your self-esteem to have the power back over your money, instead of it seemingly controlling you.

It will allow you to analyze why you think you need certain items, and whether or not you could live without them.

Plus, you'll get to see how creative you can be when you need something, but can't have it and have to make do with something you already have (or borrow, beg, or steal). Oh, no, wait. Not the stealing part.

Why 30 days?

Most people don't realize what they can achieve in such a short space of time.

Thirty days is a small enough period that you'll be able to stay with it, but large enough that you'll be able to dramatically reduce your spending. If everyone cut back their spending for just one month yearly, it's likely that they wouldn't have as many problems with their finances.

It takes between 21 and 28 days to create or break a habit. For me, thirty days is about right, and the perfect amount of time to shake bad habits up and create new healthy spending patterns.

So, by participating in this challenge for a full thirty days, you'll have a great opportunity to break bad habits and form new, better habits. And, let's face it, spending has become such a habit in our lives that most people can't account for where their money goes by the end of the week.

Buying a coffee every morning from Starbucks on the way to work – that's a habit. Making sure you get the latest magazine when it hits the stands – habit. Going to the movies every Saturday night – yes, it's a habit.

All of these are lifestyle habits that we are so accustomed to, we don't even consider that there is anything wrong with them.

I'm not saying that you can't get a coffee, or go to the movies, or even buy a magazine once the month is over.

But forcing yourself to stop spending now will show you whether you can live without your morning coffee from Starbucks (by perhaps making it at home) or whether it's something that you want to continue to do.

You'll be able to see patterns in your behavior for what they really are: habits or lifestyle choices.

And if it's something you find you could easily give up for a cheaper, or free, alternative (such as reading your favorite magazine online) then it will be worth the small sacrifice that you are making now.

This challenge is not about depriving you of what makes you happy in life, but it is about trying to find ways to reduce your spending.

So, if you cut out those expenses that have the least impact on your enjoyment and bring back only those that you truly love, you'll be richer both in pocket, and spirit.

Figure out what you can sacrifice during this month and what you can't live without. You'll be empowered by the knowledge.

What are the rules?

The rules are simple and clear: don't spend money on anything unnecessary. Basically, you want to try to limit your spending to only those items required for bare-bones survival.

Therefore you can spend money on:

- Food from the grocery store.

- Fixed Expenses - Rent or mortgage, utility bills, and other fixed bills.
- Gas/Petrol for the car - but you can only use the car for necessary trips, such as to and from work.
- Emergencies - Health/Family crises.

You cannot spend money on:

- Fast food/Dining out - it'll be home cooked meals this month only, and that includes packed lunches for work, and no store-bought coffee (yes, you'll have to make your coffee at home or work).
- Clothing/Shoes/Jewelry, unless absolutely essential – and no, going to a party doesn't count as essential.
- Homewares/Furniture - anything decorative is certainly not essential to your survival (unfortunately).
- Cell Phone (except for emergencies). All other times, you will use your home or work phone to make calls. The exception is of course, if you are already on a fixed plan whether you use the phone or not – then

you wouldn't be spending extra money anyway.

So, basically, all the fun stuff is out and the things that are essential to your survival are the only things you can spend money on. Did I mention that this challenge is going to be fun?

You can do this.

Everyone's situation may be different, but we all want control over our money.

Today, many of us are struggling. We have the recession, job losses, bankruptcies, and home foreclosures on the news daily, and credit card debt is not getting any better.

Our spending is straining relationships, and our health, due to stress. Something's got to give.

Although not spending for thirty days it isn't going to change all your financial problems, it can be the kick that you need to shake up your finances and get back on the road to financial control.

And it's only going to be for a month, anyway.

Most of you reading this book will be coming from a

similar situation, even though your lifestyles are probably quite different.

You might be a working girl looking to break your shopping habit and start saving for a deposit on your first apartment.

You might be a stay-at-home mum (like me) who has realized how out of control your finances have gotten with mounting credit card debt.

You even might be a guy (yes, guys read my books, too) who wants more control over his finances so he can plan a life together with his girlfriend (awww).

But, probably, you are frightened by how shaky the economy is, and want to do something that will fix your money situation so you won't be in trouble in the future.

Many different types of people want to detox their spending, so there will be different challenges that you'll come across according to your current lifestyle.

For example, if you are a stay-at-home mom, you might find it easier than someone who works in the city, since working with others is fraught with money leak situations from buying daily lunches, catching up with friends for coffee, or pitching in ten dollars for 'Carol's Birthday'.

Although, being able to stay at home doesn't mean it will be a walk in the park either. You'll have online shopping, the kids asking you to buy you things, and you wanting to escape to the mall for some 'me' time. You know what I'm talking about, moms.

Deciding to not spend money for thirty days is a big decision, and very often, your family and friends, while they will support your decision, may not stop spending during this time.

If they see no reasons why they should participate, it's unlikely that they will help you on your road to financial freedom.

While friends and family members who do not live with you are one thing, your spouse and children who do live with you and contribute to your overspending and debts will make this month a lot more difficult.

Sometimes it can be hard to convince your partner to stop spending for a month, even if you do have debt to tackle together. But if you can convince the whole family that this will be a fun and empowering challenge, then it will be all the more easier.

I've found that a good way to get the family on board with you is to make it like a game. Try getting a large piece of paper or calendar, and either cross the days off as you high-five each other after another successful day of no spending (like a countdown), or, if you have debt or a savings goal, write that at the top, and each time you pay off some debt or add more money to your savings goal, it will be there for the whole family to see.

Making it visual will get more of the family involved, since they'll want to take part with you. You could even make rewards for reaching certain milestones (non-monetary, of course).

Many families say it's a good chance to bond with each other by playing board games, or all having a meal at the family table, instead of eating takeaway in front of the television.

But, at the end of the day, this challenge is mostly about you. So, if they don't participate, that's okay. My family didn't stop spending during the month that I did it, although they did reduce their spending. Every little bit helps.

The Top 3 Reasons People Want to do a Spending Detox

Most people decide to do a 30-day spending detox because their current lifestyle is not getting them ahead. The top three reasons are:

1. You have mounting debt and you want to be debt-free again

2. You have a big expense/purchase coming up in the future that you want to save for.

3. You are sick of having no money left at the end of the month, and want to shake up your spending habits.

Many of us are so caught up in the everyday routine of our lives that spending becomes so automatic you can actually forget what you spend your money on.

Have you ever got to the end of the day and ask yourself where the twenty dollars that you had this morning went? That's probably because your spending has gotten to where you don't even think about it anymore. It's become subconscious habit.

This month will force you to wake up to those habits and see exactly where your money is going.

How much you'll save really depends on your current lifestyle and spending habits. Many participants also say that this is a good time to de-clutter and sell unwanted goods at places like eBay (*which we will discuss further in Chapter 5*), which can boost your finances significantly, as well.

The Best Time for a Spending Detox

While any thirty day period can work, you'll probably find it easier to begin at the start of the month and continue right through until the end of the month. But, if you want to jump in right now, then that's fine, too.

Different months are obviously going to make things easier or harder.

So, perhaps you don't want to begin in November or December over the holiday period, because there will be lots of expenses from gifts and socialising. It might be that the new year in January is the perfect time to start with your new spending resolutions.

Different months bring different challenges, and you need to be aware of these going in.

For example, in the warmer months, you will want to get

out of the house more, so you'll need to explore free options, such as walking in the park, or visiting the beach. Whereas on cold days where you are stuck inside to keep warm, you might want to avoid your usual online shopping sites, in case you get tempted.

PREPARATION IS **Key**

Before you embark on your spending detox, it's a good idea to look at your calendar to make sure that you haven't got any unexpected expenses coming up, such as birthdays, or other events that you'll need money for.

A good idea if you do have a birthday or other gift-giving occasion coming up is to purchase a gift now, before you stop spending. Otherwise, you could be in a bind when something crops up (like my pregnant friend giving birth and I didn't have a baby gift for her new bub).

Planning in advance can help make your no-spend month go much smoother, however, don't use this as an excuse to go crazy and spend big now, as that would defeat the purpose to begin with.

It's a good idea to get yourself a notebook or journal, so

you can write down those times when you really feel you want to spend money.

Don't forget to add in the reasons why you want it, as well, as this will be key to deciding if you do really want it at the end of the month.

Many our purchases are based on emotional decisions, because we think that item will make us feel better about ourselves, which rarely happens (except the immediate gratification, or shopping high, as some call it, that you may get).

Has that ever happened to you? Have you ever wanted something so badly, and purchased it, but a week later, it was no longer so important, and you were already coveting the next thing to buy? That's because it wasn't the item that you wanted, but the feeling or promise behind that item.

Many people who have done this before say that they start the month writing down everything that they plan to purchase once the month is up, but when they get to the end of the month, they realise that they've gone so long without whatever it was that they wanted, that they probably didn't want it in the first place.

If you haven't already started a budget, you can begin

one now (we will go into more detail on creating a simple budget in Chapter 7).

With all unnecessary spending out of the way this month, it allows you to concentrate on just the fixed expenses to see if there are any you can cut down, or cut out altogether.

The most important preparation that you'll need to do, which will make the month go smoothly, and allow you to get through it with ease, is your mental preparation.

CHANGING your Mindset

The hardest part of not spending money is not the actual 'not spending money' part. It's your headspace and your thoughts about money, itself. Your relationship with money will play a key role in how easy or difficult this challenge will become for you.

If you are already frugal with your money and know how to stretch a buck, then this challenge will be easy for you. However, if, like me, you are not used to going without, then things will be quite different for the month.

The easiest way to be successful is to remember the reasons for why you wanted to do this in the first place.

Write your reasons on a little card and carry it around with you, so when you are tempted to buy something that isn't a necessity; you can pull out your card and be reminded of why you wanted to do this challenge.

Some days are going to be easy, and some days are going to be difficult, but getting out of debt and reclaiming power and control over your finances and spending habits again is so worth it.

Many people who stopped spending for a month said it didn't feel as if they were going without, but that they were gaining a better understanding of themselves and their needs, and, of course, bringing them closer to freedom from debt.

For me, I simply couldn't forget the balance on our credit cards. It sat with me constantly, and, more than anything, I just wanted to get rid of it.

That's what drove me, and was the reason why I didn't find this challenge as difficult as I thought I would. I just wanted to put every cent that I earned toward reducing the amount.

If you get your head right first, then the rest will follow.

What Will You do with Your Free Time?

If you shop a lot (especially if you do it for entertainment), then the month you do your detox means that you are going to have some free time that you wouldn't normally have had.

This is another thing that you'll need to be prepared for: what are you going to do in those hours that you usually spent shopping? This might be a good time to introduce something positive and healthy into your life.

For example, you might want to take the time to exercise by walking around your city to enjoy the sights, or read that book that you've been meaning to get to. Perhaps this month is a good time to finish those craft projects or house repairs that you've never finished.

Most people complain that there are never enough hours in the day to do everything that they wanted to do, so now you are going to have a few more hours per week to allocate to starting a new hobby or catching up with long lost friends.

I used my time to de-clutter, but, as a bonus, I found I had a lot more time to play outside with my kids, whereas, before, I'd always tell them I was too busy for them. Whatever you do with your time, try to make it a positive experience so you won't feel like you are missing out by not spending money.

Before we get into some practical tips for saving and even earning some extra money this month, I'd like to delve further into why I think so many of us have gotten ourselves into financial strife. I call it the debt spending disconnect.

TWO

Debt Spending Disconnect

Our spending has gotten out of control. And it's not only consumers that are racking up immense levels of debt, our businesses and governments are in a debt crisis, as well. The problem for everyone is too much spending on credit.

No matter who you are, once you get to a point where you've borrowed to your limit and the interest rates rise above what you can afford to pay, then you have a hard time paying back the money.

Fortunately, most consumers understand this; consumer debt has been slowly reducing, rather than increasing.

This is a great sign, but we are not out of the woods, yet.

Studies by the Federal Reserve still show that the average consumer credit card debt levels in 2011 are still around $2.5K per person. (*Source: http://www.federalreserve.gov/releases/g19/Current/*).

I'm not naïve enough to assume that by the end of this thirty days that you'll be debt free, or that your spending habits will be changed for the better forever.

However, I do hope that you will at least be able to objectively look at an item and ask yourself if you really need it, or, more importantly, if you can really afford it. Being more aware of what you spend money on is an important step to taking back control of your finances.

What the thirty days did for me was make me realize how disconnected I was to the things I was buying, and how I was mostly buying them for purely superficial reasons (*this will make me look younger, this will make my house look prettier*) rather than asking why I thought buying a particular item would make me feel more worthy. Most other things I had purchased didn't fill that void, so why did I continue the cycle?

Why is it that we think 'stuff' can make us happy? Stuff is just that: stuff. Stuff to fill empty spaces, to boast about at parties. In most cases, stuff is actually hurting our self-worth by making us feel we are not good enough if we don't own it, rather than make us feel better about ourselves.

Keeping up with the Jones (or the Kardashians) is not the way to live.

I remember Oprah saying that, no matter how much money she earned, she always lived below her means so that she had money left over to save. I know what you are thinking: as if Oprah needs to worry about money. But she didn't always earn the amount she has today, and, anyway, it isn't the income that's the problem with most people, it's the spending.

It has been proven many times that an increase in wages does not help make us richer. It just allows us to spend more. It's the elastic principle, which states that your expenses will always stretch to fill your income.

Spend less than you earn, and you'll always be richer than most other people no matter what their income levels may be.

How Did We Get Into Debt?

Most people know that if you spend more money than you earn, you'll get yourself into financial trouble. Yet, when it comes to actually spending money, it seems that we ignore whether each purchase is going to put us further into debt, or not.

Not many people stand in a store and ask themselves whether they can afford the item they want to purchase. Instead, they just pick it up, try not to think about it, and hand over their credit card.

They make excuses that they will pay it once their salary comes in, or once they get their tax refund cheque. People have become disconnected to the reality that spending is causing their debt problems.

I didn't really understand how disconnected I had become, until one day, while on the spending detox, I decided to have a quick look inside a department store. I knew I couldn't spend any money in the store; I told myself that I was just there to browse and see what they had. I saw a few tops that I wanted to try on and a pair of shoes on sale. And, while I didn't purchase any of them, I started thinking about when I would come back and get them once the challenge was over.

It was then that I started to remember why I was even doing this challenge to begin with: to pay off my credit cards, and here I was, shopping in my head, and delaying any purchases for the following month.

Did I suddenly forget that I still owed ten grand on my credit cards? No, but then why did I think I deserved to buy a pair of new shoes or a new top, simply because I liked the look of it? It was clear that I was disassociating my debt from my spending.

To confuse the issue even more, I tried to reason with myself that I didn't buy anything that day not because I was thinking about my credit card balance (which was always on my mind at home, but once I got into the mall, seemed to somehow disappear), but rather that I figured I needed to finish the challenge, since I was writing a book about not spending for thirty days. I told myself it was research.

Was I really in that much denial that I also had racked up too many purchases on my credit card just because I liked the look of something?

It wasn't until that moment that I finally understood just how much of a problem most people, me included, have separating the amount that we spend and our increasing debt.

It's similar to emotional eaters, who, while they know the calorie count of most every type of food, and intellectually know what they should or shouldn't be eating, go ahead and have that extra chocolate or slice of pizza, anyway. Has emotional spending become the new disorder?

When your credit card bill comes in, does it make you want to stop spending? Of course it does! But do you? Or do you justify your purchases saying that you had a hard week and you deserve a little treat, or you want to buy the kids something because they've been so good.

Why are we doing this to ourselves?

Our culture and society is so ingrained with messages about needing more things that buying becomes a habit that is hard to break free from.

You've probably been shopping your entire life, so going cold turkey and not spend anything for thirty days may make you feel like an addict wanting to feed your addiction again by shopping.

Another reason that I believe we have such a disassociation with spending and debt is that no one uses money, anymore.

Most transactions are now done via credit or debit cards, and handing over a piece of plastic places you in a different mindset than when you actually have to count out coins and hand over real money.

It used to be that people would get their wages in an envelope and have the cash sitting in their wallets.

You remember cash, right? Those little paper notes and clinking coins that made your purse and wallet heavy? You could see as the money was being spent, until, by the end of the week, you were left with just pennies in your pocket. There was a visual clue as to how much money you were spending.

Pay checks are now directly deposited into our bank accounts, and we use cards to pay for things. We hardly ever physically see how much money we have.

It's easy to lose track of how much you are spending if you can't see it. With no visual reminder of how much each purchase, no matter how small, is adding up, you don't know how much you spend, until the credit card bill arrives.

What most people do not realise is that it's the small items that are keeping you in debt, not the larger, more expensive, items. If you have ever gotten to the end of the week, asking yourself just where your money went, then you know what I'm talking about.

A coffee here, a magazine there. If you documented everything that you spend over the course of a week, you'll probably be quite surprised on just how much you spend on small, frivolous items.

'm not suggesting that you should make a list of everything you spend, though. You won't need to write down what you spend if you are not spending anything at all.

> It's a wakeup call - most people have no idea what they are actually spending money on.

By becoming more mindful about our spending, we can take back control. It could be that, just by thinking about our purchases, we might find that we really don't need it at all, or that you already have a perfectly functional one at home that does the same job.

Being mindful about what you spend your money on is important to keeping control over it and not letting it run, or ruin you.

Deferring the Expenses

There is no doubt that everyone has expenses that they need to pay for. It might be that you need a new suit for work, or that your washing machine is leaking, and you need to get it repaired.

This challenge will not stop you from spending eventually on those items that you do need, as, inevitably, you will have to go to the store to buy the item after the month is up.

Deferring expenses isn't a bad thing. For products that you need, it is actually a good habit to get into. Not only will it give you the time to find alternatives, it will give you enough research time to find the best deal, or a better model.

There is no doubt that impulse purchases can hurt, so planning your purchases in advance is a good idea. Even better, it gets you to start thinking about how you can fit this expense into your budget, rather than just trying to figure out how you are going to pay for it once the credit card bill comes in.

Most purchases are bought on impulse, and you think you want it immediately to be happy. Deferring that purchase will make you realise that you have lived a few weeks without it already – do you really need it now?

How Can You Have More Money?

There are two ways that you can have more money: earn it, or save it. Most of the time, people try and earn it first either by taking a second job (if they can) or by finding ways to earn money from home, such as selling some of their unwanted goods on eBay.

And, if you can find extra income, then you'll be able to get out of debt much faster.

Spending less is another (and much easier) way of having more money. Too many people worry about money, and it can even cause stress-related sickness and family breakups. This is no way to live. Health and people should always come before money.

So, if you want to start saving money immediately, then not spending it to begin with is the simplest option. Putting into practice some of the tips in this book is what is going to make a difference. Just reading about it, while it might be motivating, isn't enough – you need to take action and get tough. It's boot camp, baby.

Understanding the Role Marketing and Advertising Plays on Our Spending Culture

I've just finished watching Morgan Spurlock's *The Greatest Movie Ever Sold*. It explores how prevalent advertising has become in our society from everywhere we look: on sides of buses and billboards, to appearing in television and film.

It has gotten to the point where nobody even questions ET's fondness for Reese's Pieces, or which designer bag the celebrity of the moment is holding. It seems so normal. Marketers know this, and will pay lots of money to get their product featured on television shows or to be held by celebrities.

That's why stars and social media celebs get so much free stuff - the marketers hope that they'll post photographs holding or wearing the product, and that we, the consumer, will want and buy it.

Understanding the role that marketing plays in our spending is really eye-opening, and, I think, important to keep in mind so we can realise how much we are being influenced to want so much stuff.

If you start watching ads with a critical eye, you'll see that most advertising seems to focus on either the pleasure or pain principle. You will either get pleasure and happiness from owning/using the product, or you will be able to avoid pain by using it. Both are very powerful persuaders.

But, even with all the promises of happiness, you would think that it then follows that the more stuff you have, the happier you'll become. Our general satisfaction levels and sense of happiness hasn't changed all that much since the 1950's, though. (*source: http://psychcentral.com/blog/archives/2010/04/10/5-reliable-findings-from-happiness-research/*).

> I guess the saying that money doesn't buy you happiness is absolutely correct.

This was made very clear in the film *The Economics of Happiness,* which shows how, upon taking an isolated community with little marketing influences, and 'Westernizing' it, you will find increases in conflict, financial instability, and the overwhelming belief that nothing in their lives is good enough.

This is the same community that, just years before, felt that they had meaning in their lives, more leisure time, and interacted with their community positively. Now marketing and advertising made them feel unhappy.

Where did we go wrong? If more stuff is actually making us less satisfied, increasing our debt levels, and creating health problems through stress, then why do we continue to spend?

Will Not Spending Make the Economic Situation Worse?

There will be arguments, of course, that putting an end to spending could actually make the economy worse.

I disagree.

Sure, economies are stimulated by consumption, and if nobody spent money, then companies would go out of business, and people would lose jobs. BUT, and here is the reality, this is unlikely to happen for a number of reasons.

First, it's very unlikely that suddenly one million people will stop spending for a month just because I've released this book. Most people are very reluctant to change their spending patterns; they have become accustomed to buying luxury goods. And, damn it, as if some writer would make them change their ways.

I get it. I like my stuff, too. But now I'm worried and don't want to be in debt anymore. I know my debt is relatively small compared to some, but it's still there, and it was enough to make me want to change. Most people, however, won't change.

Besides, most people who don't want to change their spending habits will not be buying this book to begin with. Those who will buy this book have either accumulated too much debt and need to shake things up, and fast, or they are sick and tired of becoming slaves to their stuff and want the insanity to stop (even if it's just for one month).

Even so, debt has a much more devastating effect on the economy than spending does. Spending does stimulate an economy, but debt stalls it in its tracks. An economy can ONLY be stimulated by spending IF the person is able to afford that spending. And using a credit card is not the way to do that.

If you look at the debt crisis around the world right now, it's because businesses and governments have spent more than they can repay. They are defaulting on their loans. Not good. More spending will not save them, just as more spending will not save us.

Something drastic needs to be done.

Besides, taking a break from spending for a while isn't a new idea. People have been trying different methods to save money and spend less for as long as they have had money problems. If you do a search online, you'll find all sorts of different websites helping you to save money, not spend, and be frugal.

During the past fifty years, the economy has been through both good and bad times. The overall level of consumer spending seems to remain stable, whether people are saving, or not.

A Change in Thinking

This challenge has a way of changing how you view money and makes you think about what you are purchasing.

Most people don't give a second thought to spending money, especially on small items, so this challenge, even after it is over, should help you be more mindful about what you are buying.

The small items are the real killers here, because, more often than not, they are unnecessary. They are like those empty calories that you don't even think about unless you are on a diet. But a can of Coke here and an iPod music purchase there means nothing to most people, and they will make the purchases without even thinking about it.

By freezing your spending, you will be forced to think about all of your purchases again. It may be that just paying attention to what you are buying is enough to stop the debt spending disconnect.

The sad fact is that most people spend more than they earn. Perhaps not every week, but with unexpected bills, subconscious spending, and the strive to look more affluent than they really are, generally, most people spend more than they bring in.

Marketing and advertising play a large role in the problem, but most of the time, it's just become the norm to try and gratify our wants immediately, rather than save up for something, or go without. So we use our credit cards, dip into our mortgages, and end up going into debt to pay for things that we shouldn't.

At the end of the day, being in debt is a situation that we can't blame others for. It's our own fault and by taking responsibility for that, we can take back control.

Sure, I know that circumstances can contribute to bad financial situations, such as losing your job, having your stock investments dissolve, or getting scammed out of cash. Sometimes life sucks.

But you can't be a victim here, you need to take the control back and start to help yourself. The good news (and the bad news) is that **you** need to be responsible for getting your debt and spending back on track.

Consumerism has become such a prevalent way of life today that people go to the mall just for entertainment.

Since when did shopping become a way to waste time? With the millions of advertising and marketing messages being thrown at us everyday to be younger, sexier, smarter, or thinner, it has many of us believing that we need these extra things in our lives just to fit in. These messages have made us think that we are not good enough just as we are.

This is rubbish, of course.

We need to remember that people are not what they own. People are who they are, regardless of how much they have.

THREE

Saving Money

Now we can get to the nuts and bolts of this month. The real reason why you are doing it is to save some money by not spending. And, for most of the month, you'll do that easily, simply by cutting out all your unnecessary spending.

However, you might want to take it a step further and see if you can be frugal and save even more money by cutting back on those expenses that you do need to pay for.

Because housing costs are generally fixed (and I'm not about to suggest you move house or look for a cheaper mortgage during this month) it's really only the variable expenses that you'll be able to cut out or cut back on.

This chapter will look at where you can save a few extra dollars on transportation, food, utility bills, and entertainment during your spending detox.

Saving Money on Transportation

While transportation costs can include plane trips and other holiday travel, I'll assume that for most of your spending detox month, you'll be at home and not jetting off to an exotic location. That leaves public transport and gas/petrol costs for your car that you want to try and cut back on.

You will still need to use your car this month to get to/from work and to/from the grocery store (unless you already use public transport or even better - walk) so, looking for ways to save money means that you are going to have to get creative.

Your first option is to see if anyone from your workplace lives in your neighbourhood so that you can suggest carpooling. If you can get a few people involved, it can be a good way to save money and have a good workplace gossip on the way to work.

If you would rather not befriend any of your co-workers, then it's time to become a detective and find out which days the gas station has cheaper prices. Generally gas prices are lower at the middle of the week and get higher at the end of the week and weekends when most people fill up for their weekend trips.

Keep an eye (or a diary) on your local station to see when they have their best prices, and fill up on those days. Some apps will do this for you too.

When going to the grocery store, try and go at quieter times of the day so that you can find a park closer to the store. Driving around the car park, looking for an empty space, uses up petrol, and, besides, who wants to shop at the busiest time? Not me!

If you want to get super green, you can even bike or walk to work (if you work close enough) so that you are not even using your car. Weather permitting, of course.

While these small tips are not going to make too much of an impact in just one month, if you continue them over the course of the year. you'd be able to save a lot. It's definitely worth trying to see where you can save on car and gas costs.

Food Shopping

Using the car is not my biggest expense, since I work from home and generally only use the car to go the store a few times a week. For us, food shopping was a budget killer.

Prior to doing the spending detox, it was not unusual for me to go into the grocery store just to pick up a couple of items, and walk out having spent well over $100, and find I needed to return to the store within a day or two because we were out of food, again.

There was a time when I tried to buy only those items that were on special, purchase meat in bulk to save money, or even go at the end of the day when the store would mark down fresh items. But truth be told, that requires a lot of commitment - something that our busy family just doesn't have time for.

Now, there is nothing wrong with buying things on sale - if you use them already - but buying just for the sake of getting something cheaper does not always work out to be the best cost-effective solution.

To be fair, my rules don't restrict what you can or cannot put into your trolley to buy for your family, so, if you need a box of pop tarts, who am I to argue? But, having a closer look at what you do spend can help you to save more and become debt free faster.

I'm not about to give you a bare bones survival shopping list where you can only eat noodles and toast for the month (who needs all those carbs anyway?) so, instead I'll share two of the strategies that worked best for me in reducing my grocery bills. I call them the *three item cutback* and *stepping down a branding level.*

THE THREE ITEM Cutback

The first strategy came about because I didn't want to stop buying the groceries that we used, but I did want a way to save money on them. So, it was time to put on the detective hat (or tiara) and see which three items were the most expensive on my grocery list each week.

Once you've found these three products, the goal is to see if you can cut those costs in half, or more, by finding different brands, alternatives, or source out where they are the cheapest. Then, when you've accomplished cutting back on these three items, look at your bill the following week and pick the next three most expensive items. Work at cutting those back

And so on and so on.

The sneaky way that this can work is that the family, who often doesn't want any drastic changes to family meals and snacks, often won't even notice that anything has changed, since you are cutting back gradually.

For my family, I recognised that the three most expensive items in my trolley were laundry detergent, nappies (diapers), and expensive beef steaks.

The laundry detergent was the easiest to fix, since I wasn't loyal to one particular brand, but tended to choose premium powders, as I thought these cleaned our clothes the best.

The first week on the detox, I purchased a mid range brand that was on sale for half the price. And, while that did cut back by about five dollars, I knew that I could do better, and went online to find a brilliant, and super cheap, laundry powder recipe that you can make at home.

Frugal Tip

Normally, I'm not a 'make it at home' type. Making your own laundry powder to me is a symbol that things are dire. And, since I want to keep things fun and simple, I wasn't sure whether this would really fit the bill. But, since this only had three ingredients, and claimed it would clean clothes better than the premium brands, I figured it would be worth a go. It was surprisingly easy too, and here is the recipe:

- 1 bar of laundry soap (sometimes called pure soap)

- 1 cup washing soda (also called soda ash or sodium carbonate)

- ½ cup borax

That's it. Other recipes also said that you could add one small box of baking soda to make it extra effective, and I ended up taking this advice to be sure that all the stains would come out. I also added a few drops of lemon essential oil, since I love citrusy fragrances – but, of course, that's entirely optional.

Now, to make the powder up, you grate the soap and combine it with the borax and washing soda. That's it. Sounds easy enough (as long as you don't grate your fingers, which I have a habit of doing sometimes). There were also some suggestions that you could put the washing soda crystals into the food processor to make it more fine. At first, I thought this was weird (who wants to put soap in your food processor?) but, actually, I wash my food processor with dish soap all the time, so it wasn't so weird, after all. For storage, use an airtight container. I have a front loader, so I used 2 teaspoons per wash. Use 3 teaspoons if you have a top loader.

It was actually really easy, and even kind of fun, in a weird make-it-yourself way. Plus, it took no more than five minutes, which is an added bonus to the first fact that it's super cheap!

THE NEXT ITEM on my list was nappies (diapers). This one, I struggled quite a lot with, since I really didn't want to stop buying the premium brand, having had bad leakage experiences with cheaper brands. So, I didn't change brands at all, I just shopped around for the best prices.

While I wasn't able to cut this expense to half, I did save a few dollars off the price, which I was satisfied with.

Some might tell you that using cloth nappies (diapers) would be a less expensive alternative too, but I disagree. The electricity and washing that is needed on them (especially if you can't line dry them) can be just as expensive.

The last and most expensive item on our list was beef steaks.

This was going to be tricky, considering Husband wouldn't appreciate being served a vegetarian meal in its place (although I would be perfectly happy).

So, instead, I purchased slightly thinner steaks: less meat overall, but not enough that anyone would notice. And, yes, I also looked for special prices and promotions, as well.

The next week, I had to tackle cereal bar snacks for the kids (and Husband), cappuccino coffee mix for me (sad face, thinking I'd have to cut back on that), and salmon (who needs omega 3, anyway?).

So, what are the three most expensive items on your list?

STEPPING Down a Branding Level

Stepping down a branding level sounds kind of weird, but it's actually pretty simple.

There are generally four levels of branding for each range of products:

1. the premium brand (usually the most expensive),

2. the manufacturer's brand (iconic everyday brands most of us use and know)

and two different levels of supermarket brands, usually consisting of a

3. high-quality generic brand, and a

4. budget-friendly generic brand.

Most people suggest that you should go directly to buying the cheapest generic products if you want to cut down, but I've found that this isn't desirable for most people, as they have been used to certain products. So, instead of dropping right to the bottom of the brands, just go down one level.

If you usually buy the premium brands, go down to the mid-level manufacturer's brands. Or, if you use the manufacturer's brands, try the supermarket high-quality generic brand. That way, it's not so much a shock going from premium to no-frills generic in one fell swoop.

If you find that you can handle the level below where you usually buy, then you can try going down an extra level, again, and see how that fits.

More Grocery Store Tips for Saving Money

Grocery stores are designed for you to spend money. The layout of the store makes it so that you have to pass most of the impulse buys, like chocolate bars and magazines, which are conveniently located at the counter.

The soft, hypnotic music, which scientific studies have shown, actually does slow you down so that you look at every shelf (and are therefore more persuaded to buy something on impulse).

The longer the supermarkets can keep you in the store, the more likely you are to spend money on them. Knowing that going in means you can avoid many of the potential money drainers located around the store.

The best piece of advice (and one that most people tell you because it works) is to have a list and stick with it.

Not having a list often means that you'll either pick up items that you don't necessarily need, or forget something important, so you'll have to come back to the store again to get it (and be further tempted to buy extra items).

There are lots of great menu-planning sites online, or

you can write your own family menu plan based on meals that your family likes to eat.

Involve the family and make it fun so that each night, someone gets to pick what the family eats (which is a sneaky way to get them to help out on 'their' night).

Make sure you allocate enough food for breakfast, lunch, and dinner, as well as snacks and drinks.

Saving Money on Utility Bills

Another huge expense in my household are the utility bills, and, in particular, the electricity and gas accounts for heating and cooling.

During both the coldest days in the winter and the hottest days in the summer, our heating and cooling is on all the time, both day and night (yes, I know this is bad for the environment, I'm working on it).

So, it wasn't really a surprise to get the latest bill, which showed our quarter expenditure on electricity was over $800. That's more than $8 a day. Yikes.

Now, there is no way I'm going to recommend that you freeze or swelter in uncomfortable temperatures inside your homes, but, by being mindful of what you are using in your home can help reduce your bills greatly.

You have probably already heard most of the tips for saving money on electricity.

The most common being to turn off appliances at the power points so they are not left on standby, lower your thermostat a few degrees in the winter, and raise it in the summer so that it's a constant temperature (rather than blasting the heat when you are cold, and cranking the air conditioner up to max in the summer).

I don't have any superb tips that are going to make any significant difference in just one month.

Unless you can live without power, altogether, and, if you can, then more power to you (pun intended).

Personally, I can't live without electricity and gas, so I had to come up with solutions that didn't cost anything, but that also didn't impact our lifestyles too much.

The method that worked best for our family was to go through with an 'audit'. I did this by tackling each room, one at a time. I started with the bedrooms. since these would probably be the easiest to change.

Take a notepad and write down everything that is used

in that room. Obviously you'll have lights in there, but how many do you have (and, more importantly, how many do you need?)

In our main bedroom, I found that I didn't use the overhead lights that often, and preferred the bedside lamps to light the room for reading.

While I couldn't remove the overhead lights, I listed it as something to be mindful about not using whenever possible (rather than just turning them on out of habit every time I walked into the room). Also, switching your light bulbs to energy efficient models will help save a few bucks, as well.

In the kitchen, it was clear that most of the appliances I had plugged in didn't need to be 'on' at the power point. Why I kept the toaster plugged in all day and night is anyone's guess. Laziness, perhaps?

Anyway, it was time for the toaster to live in the drawer where it belongs, and to be taken out only when needed. Plus, it cleared up the kitchen counters and made them look neater: another bonus!

In the laundry, I had to put a ban on the clothes dryer. When wind and sunshine can dry clothes just as well as the dryer (and give clothes that nice fresh fragrance) it doesn't take a lot of extra time to hang them outside.

Don't have a clothes line? Can you hang them on folding clothes racks, perhaps? The clothes drying rack can also be used inside if you don't have the space outside (or the weather has turned against you).

Now, obviously, none of these changes are going to make significant cost savings in the short term (especially not in just one month), but, over time, they can add up, and every dollar saved is better than a dollar earned.

Saving Money by Swapping Goods

Just because you are not going to be doing any general spending within your no-spend month (right!?) that doesn't mean that you can't have anything new (or newish). There are some great places where you can actually get stuff for free. No kidding!

There are lots of different free and swap-type websites, such as freecycle.org, where you can either list your unwanted goods, or take someone else's stuff (as long as you pay for postage/shipping costs) all for nada.

It's worth checking out these sites if you are looking for

something in particular, as you'll be amazed at what some people are giving away.

Apart from freecycle.org, here is a list of some of the more popular swap sites:

paperbackswap.com

bookmooch.com

swaptree.com

swapadvd.com

swapacd.com

Saving Money on Entertainment

Entertainment is another thing that many of us spend money on. While I go into more detail on things you can do with your buddies in the next chapter, for now, doing simple things like looking in your local paper or local area online can often bring back lots of free entertainment that is going on in your community.

A local theatre group might be holding free performances in the town hall, or it could just be as simple as going to a park and having a picnic.

In our local area, they often have fireworks nights with entertainment for the kids on special occasions, such as Christmas, New Years Eve, and Australia Day. All free (except for any food that you might purchase, which, if you are budgeting, you'd bring your own).

I think that covers most of the things that you might encounter on your no-spend month. Really, it's about being creative and seeing if there are free alternatives to anything that you might need that won't cost you money.

Just because you are not spending money doesn't mean you have to sit at home with the lights out (because that would be just sad). There are still plenty of ways to have some fun and keep things interesting.

FOUR

CHAPTER

4

How to Deal with Unexpected Expenses

"One cannot plan for the unexpected" - *Aaron Klug, Physicist*

THE MONTH IS GOING great so far, and you are starting to get ahead financially. You really think that you can do this and get through the month fairly pain-free. And then it happens. Bam! You need to spend money on something that you weren't planning for.

There is a very good chance that during your thirty-day spending detox, you'll have unexpected expenses that you may not have thought about ahead of time, causing you to consider breaking your no-spending rule.

Life happened. Even the most organized person has unexpected expenses that they don't see coming. It sucks, but its reality.

The most common of these is socializing with friends, gifts, and repairs around the home.

I'm not talking about real emergencies, like if your car breaks down, or one of your family members needs to see a doctor, (which are allowed, and should definitely be attended to) but those non-essential expenses that you find yourself in where spending money is expected.

What do you do at times like these? Do you buckle and pay up, delay the expense, or be a hard ass and say that there's no way you'll give in?

Gifts

Probably the most common expenses that you don't budget for are gifts that you need to buy. Birthdays, anniversaries, John's last day at work, and so on. Sometimes you might just want to buy a gift for someone as a thank you for doing a service or good deed.

But, ask yourself whether any of these expenses are

REALLY unknown. Most often, you know in advance about upcoming birthdays and anniversaries. And, if that's the case, you can plan ahead so that you don't break your no-spend month.

For me, it was my friend who had a baby during the time I gave up spending. Of course, I knew she was pregnant, and I also knew approximately when she was due, but for some reason, I didn't think about buying her a gift until she actually HAD the baby. Which she did, of course, right smack bang in the middle of my not-spending money month.

Now, if you weren't organized like me, then you are going to have to be really creative. Perhaps you could find something on freecycle.org, offer a handmade gift (baked cookies are always welcome) or even do something helpful for a gift (like doing her laundry while she looks after the baby).

If you have gift cards that haven't been used yet, or loyalty points on your credit card just waiting to be used, it might be a good time to cash them in for a gift if you can't wait.

Many people's points accumulate and eventually expire,

so, if you don't have anything already planned with your points, then go ahead and gift it up.

Or, you can take a stand and just not buy gifts at all (nor ask for any in return). This is a perfectly reasonable option, especially if you are in debt and are doing this challenge to get yourself out of real financial strife.

That might be a little harsh, but making someone else feel better for the few minutes it takes to open a gift and say "ooh" or "ahh" isn't worth getting yourself into further debt for.

Obviously this isn't going to be a permanent solution: eventually your kids will ask why Santa doesn't visit them, anymore, and you can only use the excuse that they've been on the naughty list for so many years until they catch on.

SOCIALIZING with friends

Hanging out with your buddies is another expense, which, while you probably don't plan ahead for it, is inevitable, since our social culture usually dictates doing something where money is required.

Whether that's hanging out at the shopping mall, going to a bar, or catching a movie together, spending money is a big part of socializing. So, you might think that this month, you are going to have to ditch your friends and become a lonely old hermit.

Hopefully that won't be the case, but you are going to have to be a little bit creative. If the weather is great, then meeting at a park for a picnic, or at the beach for some rays are great free options.

Instead of going out to a bar or for dinner, invite your friends over to your house and they can bring the wine! Perhaps have a movie night in, instead of going out.

Many people think that they don't want to tell their friends that they are doing a spending detox for fear that they'll be laughed at, and that their friends won't understand, but you might want to give your buds a little more credit.

Perhaps they want to pull back on the spending a little, as well, and won't mind doing some free alternatives with you. Or, perhaps they'll go the whole hog and join you in not spending money for a whole month. You could find lots of different free activities that you can do together that way.

The following are some ideas for free socializing.

Scavenger Hunt.

Remember those good old-fashioned scavenger hunts? You could add a new twist to the concept and explore your own city at the same time. Friends did one recently and had tasks like finding old train tickets (fairly easy at a nearby train station) to counting how many windows a certain building had. Five couples joined in, and it was a race to find the items and fill in the clues.

The hunt took over an hour to complete, and they had a huge picnic at the end. They are still talking about how much fun it was. It will be just like your own mini Amazing Race.

Game Night

No, game nights don't have to be lame; they can actually be a lot of fun! Especially if you choose games where people have to do silly things (like charades) or draw (Pictionary). And, if you have a glass or wine, or two (if you drink) things can get really funny.

If you or the kids have a Wii or Xbox, then you could even play one of the party games on these. There are some really funny games that groups can play and interact with on consoles these days, so they really aren't just for the kids.

Replicate Your Usual Outing at Home

My friend, Kate, likes to catch up for coffee to complain about our husbands, so when I said that I couldn't make it for one month (I explained my reasons why) she set her porch up to look like a coffee shop. She invited me over and even had menus on the table (there was only one type of coffee and one type of cake on the menu, though).

It was lots of fun, and we've continued to have coffee dates at each other's houses since. It's much cheaper, and you don't have to whisper when you gossip. Win win!

SCHOOL COSTS

If you have children at school, you'll know how often the kids come home with forms for various school excursions or fundraisers, and it may seem that all the school seems to want from you is money all the time. As if paying tuition wasn't enough (for those schools that still have it).

Very often, you can't plan ahead for these, unless your school is very organized and gives you prior notice of when such expenses might occur. Without incurring the wrath of your son or daughter, who won't understand why you are not giving them money to go to the packing factory, it may be that you are going to have to fork out for it.

School fundraisers can be difficult, but, fortunately, you are not required to buy whatever products (usually candy) that are being offered. It's not the school's fault; often they really do need money for a new gymnasium. But that doesn't help when you are trying to tighten your belt.

The best you can do is try and help sell your child's fundraising goods to other people. If you work, then take the box of chocolates (or whatever) and place it in the reception area so everyone knows they are there). Dad could do this at his workplace, as well.

If there are any items left over, then it's time to make a visit to the grandparents for the last of the box. Don't feel guilty that you are involving the in-laws; that's what they are there for, right?

CHARITY DONATIONS

Most of us are a charitable bunch, and will often place a dollar in a busker or beggar's tin at the subway. We might even give a few bucks to the church charity that comes to our door asking for help for a family in need.

But right now, you need to ask yourself whose need is more important. Obviously the reason you are doing the spending detox is because you are in debt, or your spending is out of control. Concentrating on that will help put in perspective that you need to help yourself first. After all, charity begins at home.

But, if you do want to help out, then volunteering is a no-cost way of doing your charitable duty. In fact, volunteering within an organization could be a better way of helping your chosen charity, since most people are much more willing to give up their money than their time.

By helping out hands-on, you can really feel good that you are doing something worthwhile for the people involved.

Emergencies

If there are true emergencies while you are doing your

no-spend month, then there is no question - you must pay for them.

However, sometimes it might be health, repair, or family-related, but not truly an emergency. And what you consider essential may not be essential to someone else.

What would you do if you had a family member rock up on your doorstep saying that they need $1,000, or else their car will be repossessed? Is that a necessary expense, or is it not your problem?

Perhaps your toaster oven is on the blink and you need a new one. Can it wait until next month, or can it be repaired?

Working out what you can avoid or delay up front will help you decide whether the expense is a true necessity and needs to be paid, or whether you can go without (or tell your family member to go get a job and pay for it themselves).

How Being More Organized Can Help Save Money

Whatever the unexpected expense may be, it probably won't be such an issue if you are more organized. By planning ahead for those costs, you can budget it in or pay upfront so you don't have to compromise your spending plans.

Perhaps you might even be able to delay the purchase for the following month. I did this when my friend had her baby, as we weren't planning on visiting them straight away (they live a good driving distance away).

Instead of sending a gift in the mail, I waited until we saw them in person a few months later. This actually turned out much better for both me and her, because I knew in advance what gifts she had already received, so I didn't double up on something she already had.

We already know that having a shopping list and sticking to it can help you stick to your budget when it comes to groceries, but being organized can also help in other ways.

Knowing when certain bills are due and paying them on time will avoid any late fees that you might incur. And, anyway, who wants to pay the utility companies anything more than your fair share? Plus, you have more time to research gifts and find good deals if you start a few months before the actual event.

Polly did this for an upcoming wedding that she and her

partner were attending. *"We knew about it months in advance, because they had been talking about the month that they wanted their wedding every time we caught up, so it was just a matter of looking around and waiting for the sales to get the perfect gift at 50% off, well before they walked down the aisle."*

Plus, she managed to get a great outfit on eBay that was an original, and a bargain to boot.

Giving yourself plenty of time means you are not rushing to grab the first thing you see, and it will save you not only time, but lots of stress, as well.

Emergency Funds

So far, we've mostly been talking about those unexpected expenses that come up that you can probably avoid fairly easily by either delaying them or making do with what you have.

However, as I've mentioned, there are plenty of expenses that might arise where you actually do need to pay for them, such as medical expenses, car breakdowns, emergency repairs, and so on.

I've already said that if these come up, then you do need to go ahead and pay for them.

That is all well and good if you have the money to do so, but what happens if you don't? What happens if you have no emergency fund set up and have to use your credit card again?

Unfortunately, this is a sad reality for many people. In a recent survey by The National Foundation for Credit Counselling (NFCC) of nearly 3,000 people, it was found that 64% of Americans don't have $1,000 or more in an emergency account to cover unexpected expenses, should they arise.

This is a big reason why many people are getting into financial trouble, because they don't have the resources to handle things when they crop up (which we've already established they do - it's life).

So, where do most people get the money to pay for these emergencies? Most respondents to the survey said that they would either have to ask friends or family for a loan, or use credit cards to pay for it. If that wasn't an option, then they would have to cut back on other living expenses to save up to cover the costs.

I'm actually not surprised by this at all. Before I started

getting interested in money, I had no savings. If anything major came up, I would use credit cards to cover myself until I got my next pay check.

It wasn't until I realised how risky this was and started getting interested in improving my financial situation that I started putting away a few dollars here and there for such emergencies.

Once this month is over and you decide to continue living below your means, then it's probably a very good time to start thinking about starting an emergency fund, if you don't have one already.

You've already shown yourself that you can live frugally for thirty days, so it shouldn't take you too long to save up $2,000 or more and place it into a savings account.

Once you have the account set up with some funds in it, you'll need to write a list for yourself of what potential emergencies you would use that money for. That way, you'll have a guideline so you don't take it out for anything that isn't really important.

Try and keep the savings account separate from your regular spending account so that you know exactly what that money is for. It helps if you shop around for a high interest account so you can earn interest on your money while it is sitting there.

Having a bit of cash set aside for when you need it will give you peace of mind that you won't be left out of pocket if the worst happens. And that's got to make you feel good.

The reason that I think you should have $2,000 in your savings account is because research has shown that this is the average amount of unexpected expenses that most families can expect during a year.

The study showed that the biggest breakdown of what were the top unexpected expenses, 34% are usually medical in nature, 24% due to vehicle repairs, 20% for expenses around the home, or business, and 9% for family expenses (and sometimes higher, if you have children).

Of course, most financial planners will tell you that you need a year's worth of expenses in your emergency fund so that if you lose your job, you've got twelve months to get back on your feet. While that's a good long term goal, just getting enough in there to cover basic emergencies can be enough to begin with.

What to Do if You DO Spend Money during the Detox

Unexpected expenses are a fact of life, and they will occur whether you are doing your spending detox, or not. There may be some times when you absolutely have to pay and you can't delay it until the following month. If that's the case, then go ahead. It's obviously a necessary expense.

Knowing what is important and what you can do without will help you get through this month much easier.

If you do end up spending money, then don't feel guilty. Just get back to not spending again as soon as you can. You didn't fail; you just had a little hiccup, and no doubt learned from the experience. In fact, this whole month will be one big learning journey, whether unexpected expenses crop up, or not.

Remember why you are doing this challenge in the first place, and that is probably to curb your spending and get out of debt. While it would be great if you can do the whole month with no extra spending, it's also a fact of life that unexpected challenges come up. Deal with them quickly and get back to your detox.

Think about the possibility of such a situation arising again. What would you do differently? What could you have done differently last time? This is just a small step in changing your spending habits. Don't make it any bigger than it needs to be.

You are doing great.

FIVE

CHAPTER
5

How to Make Extra Money

S o far, we've talked mainly about how to save money by not spending, cutting back, and being as frugal as possible during the thirty-day detox. However, if you are on a limited income, there is only so much that you can cut back on.

While the majority of this challenge IS about learning to spend less, finding ways to help boost your savings or get out of debt faster means that you might want to bring in some extra income. So, this chapter will go over some of the quick ways that you can earn some extra cash this month to help give your funds a well-deserved boost.

Let's start with the most obvious first.

What to Do With Your De-cluttered Goods

If you've already been de-cluttering during this month, then some of those unwanted goods might be able to earn you a penny, or two, to help fatten the piggy bank.

There are two main ways to get rid of your stuff for the most profit and that is either on eBay or by having a garage sale. There are advantages and disadvantages of both methods and which you choose will come down to which suits your style (or space) better.

EBAY

Selling unwanted goods on eBay is nothing new, and many people even make full time businesses from it. This can be especially profitable if you have quirky or unusual items, or even better - old collector's items that are hard to come by. But, of course, if you are like most people and don't have a stack of Phantom original comics in the basement, then selling ordinary everyday items can be lucrative as well.

Before you start, evaluate each item individually and do some research on eBay to see if there are already lots of similar items. Check what the going rate is.

You can also see what the items have sold for by checking the box marked 'Completed Listings' under the 'Show Only' menu in the left-hand menu bar. That's a good way to see which auctions did the best. Take note of what they wrote in the title and description, as well as what they started their bidding price at.

You'll notice that the auctions that go for the highest usually have a lot of keywords in the title that people might be searching for, so if you have something that might be called a few different names, then try and get them all in the title.

For example, which do you think would come up in more searches: 'Disney Playing Cards' or 'Collectible Disney Trade Cards with Mickey Mouse'?

Obviously you are only limited to 55 characters, but it's a good idea to use as many as you can to get more searchable keywords in there. Because you are limited in space, it's also not a good idea to put attention-grabbing symbols, such as "!!@@LOOK@@!!" It uses up valuable keyword space, and has been proven to actually lower sales results, since people perceive it to be spam-like.

Taking a good photo is also important to a good auction result. You don't have to be a professional photographer, but there are few simple tricks that you can use to make your item look more appealing.

Good lighting is the first one, and probably the most important. So try and photograph your item somewhere bright - even outside, if that helps.

Using an uncluttered background will also help your item stand out. It doesn't have to be against a plain wall, though.

When I was selling cosmetics on eBay, I'd photograph them sitting on the bathroom sink (I had really good lighting in the bathroom) and, while the product was the main focus, it looked nice having it in context.

Pricing strategies can also help boost the price of items. Now, while most people go onto eBay looking for a bargain, you need to find the right balance between what people are prepared to pay, and the minimum that you are willing to accept. Many different strategies say that starting at 0.99 cents is a good method, because you'll get more people interested and bidding on your auction, which quickly escalates the price, since no one wants to be out-bid.

It's rare that a good item will sell for the minimum

amount you set, and you can save money on fees by starting it at the lower price.

Of course, if you really don't want to start your auction so low, then start at the absolute minimum that you'll accept, and then whatever it goes above that is a bonus.

Finally, run your auctions for the full seven days to get the maximum eyeballs on your auction as possible. That should ensure the best result.

GARAGE SALES

If you can't stand the thought of spending hours photographing, writing descriptions, and then mailing your items out, then you could try and get rid of everything in one fell swoop with a garage sale.

You will still need to plan ahead, though, and decide how you are going to display your goods (on trestle tables, hanging clothes on racks, in baskets, etc.) and how you will price items.

It's a good idea to get a fanny pack (bum bag) that attaches around your waist so you can collect money right wherever the person is, rather than sending them to a 'payment' area.

Negotiation is par for the course at garage sales, so expect people to haggle over your goods.

Unlike eBay, it's best to start a little higher that you would actually like at a garage sale, so that when people haggle you down, you'll still be getting a fair price (and they will think they got a bargain!).

There will likely be many goods left over at the end of the sale, so you'll need to decide what you want to do with any leftover products. Do you send them to your local charity? Dump them? Or will you then try and sell THOSE leftovers on eBay?

HOBBIES / Mini Businesses

Often times when you start seeing some cash roll in from using places like eBay; you'll start to look around your house at what else you can sell. This is usually where people think that they might like to make a mini business out of their hobbies (e.g. craft projects) or find more items to sell (e.g. used books) and make some regular cash.

I did this for about a year by going to a big luxury brand cosmetic warehouse and buying their trial-size and out-of-stock products at super cheap prices, and then selling these items on eBay. I used to make around $50 or $60 a week doing this.

There are many really talented, crafty people selling their quilts, knitted hats, and handmade teddy bears online, and they're doing really well, too.

There might be something that you could do to build a mini business, as well, whether that's going to garage sales to find good items to sell on eBay, or by making original one off's yourself.

If the business gets big enough then you could even sell items on your own website or take your craft items to consignment shops to make more money.

PART TIME / Casual Jobs

Often the first thing people think of doing when they need extra cash is to take a part time or second job to bring in extra income.

In theory, this might seem like a good idea, and, if you can find jobs easily enough, then it's a good option. However, with unemployment rates so high, it can be difficult to even find good part time jobs, and many people who can't get full time employment are snapping them up just so they can make ends meet.

It's no longer as easy as giving your resume to the local supermarket for night filling anymore. It's a lot of work finding decent, well-paying, part time work.

You'll also need to factor in the time you'll be doing the job, and if it will interfere with your current work and/or family life to decide whether it's worth it.

If you can find a good part time job, then great, go for it. But be aware that it isn't so easy to get these second jobs anymore due to the bad economy.

MAKING Extra Cash Online

Making money online has got a bit of a bad reputation, but, like anything, there are completely legitimate and ethical ways to do this, and there are outright scams, as well.

Personally, I love the opportunity the internet has brought to allow everyday people to reach an audience worldwide to promote their products or services.

There are many different ways to make money online, so I'll go over some of the easiest ways to get started here.

Obviously you are going to need a computer and an internet connection, which I'll assume you already have, or can access nearby, (although trying to earn an income online probably won't work if you have to go to the library everyday to get online).

Fiverr.com

If you've not done anything before online and you just want to get a chance to earn some quick cash, then there is a great little site called fiverr.com that you can join and offer to do something for five dollars. You could hold up a sign with someone's website address on it, sing happy birthday for someone, or knit a little doll's scarf. The options are only limited by your imagination (and if you have a look at what some people are offering, you'll see that there are so many weird and wonderful things that people will offer to have you do for money).

So, if someone buys your 'gig,' then you make five bucks. (Actually, you only get four bucks, because Fiverr takes one dollar as their fee.)

Now, this money isn't going to make you rich, but if you could sell, say, five gigs a week, then that's $20 more than you would have had otherwise. $20 a week over six months is $520, which would be a nice little boost to your savings account.

Probably the most used services on Fiverr are the writing and business promotion services that people offer. If you don't mind writing a 500-word article for $4, and you can write a half way decent article on the topic of the user's choosing, then you could do very well.

Guru.com / elance.com

Guru and eLance are freelance websites that you can find work on or can use to advertise your services. Again, they are mostly geared toward business promotion, writing, and office management-type jobs, but you'll earn more money here than you would on places like Fiverr.

For a good writer, a 500-word article (for example) might reach $10 or more (which is more than double what you'd get on Fiverr) but it is harder to get work here, as many people are competing for different jobs.

The good thing about these freelance sites is that once you do get a job and do good work for the client, then they will no doubt give you more and more work, and it can build very quickly.

Surveys

There are many different survey sites that will offer you money for filling out their questionnaires. I have to be honest with you, mostly, these are a waste of your time. Usually the money that you make isn't worth the amount of effort that you put into it, and, for the most part, companies just want your email address.

If you do decide to fill out surveys, then definitely use a throwaway email address that is not linked to your personal email, because the spam from using this email will quickly mount up.

In my opinion, there are better ways to make a buck online than this.

Blogging

You might have heard about different bloggers that earn upwards of six figures simply by writing their thoughts down on a simple blog. While this CAN happen, it's very unlikely to happen within a month (and possibly not even for the first year).

Now, I'm a big believer in using the internet to make money online, but it's a big learning curve to understand the difference between business blogging, optimizing your website for search engine traffic, pay per click traffic, or social media traffic.

Business blogging is a lot different than just writing about things that you are interested in (although the two can be combined). For example, if your hobby is making boots for dogs (which actually sounds like a great business idea, but I digress) then you need to understand how to write in a way that will earn you money (say from writing 'how to' guides or selling 'products' rather than just talk about the types of things that you like.

Of course, once you do understand the difference and want to pursue it, then this is really where the most money to be made online is.

If you want to take this path, then I must warn you first that if you start looking online for 'make money online tips and tricks', then you are going to find a lot of promises of making thousands overnight, or easy money for virtually no work.

These sales-type marketing messages are everywhere, and it'll only cost you $97 to get the 'secrets' so you, too, can be a success.

Stay skeptical.

Usually, if someone wants you to pay a huge price for any 'secrets' to success, then the person selling the secrets is the one making the money - not the person buying the eBook or course.

Sure, there are a lot of well-meaning online marketers who have legitimate products and are just trying to make a living, as well, but, for the most part, it's all hype designed to lure in newbies who are struggling to get ahead.

Very often, you can find the same information that they are offering in their products for free, or for low cost, on places like Amazon, written by proven authors.

Okay, so now I've got that disclaimer out of the way, how DO you make money online by blogging?

There are two ways to do this: the absolute free way, and the way which will cost you a few dollars to set up, but has the potential to earn you more money in the long term.

Let's talk about the free ways first.

ARTICLE SITES:

Article sites are just what they sound like: you provide the content and either get paid a flat fee or share advertising revenue that the article makes.

Probably the best known of these is hubpages.com (revenue sharing) and iwriter.com (flat fee). Although there are many others.

On each of these sites, you create an account and then write articles on whatever you like. Then the site will put advertising on your page for which you earn a percentage of the profits or pay you per word count.

So, if you write an article on how to prune large trees, you might want to recommend a book from Amazon that deals with this subject matter, and if someone buys that book from your page, you'll get a commission.

Many people who start at these places claim that they can make up to $1,000 or more a month from writing lots of different articles and promoting products, but again, this is not the norm.

It can be a good place to get a feel for affiliate marketing, though, so that you can learn what works and what doesn't.

Usually, the most profitable types of articles on these

sites are 'how to' informational articles, or product review-type articles.

You can make these as short or as long as you want, but generally longer articles do better. For both sites (and others like it) it pays to read their requirements, help pages and instructions on getting started.

YOUR OWN WEBSITE:

Having your own website is really where you should head if you are serious about building a business online. But that's not free, since you'll need to buy a domain name and hosting for your site.

Your domain name can be anything you like (as long as it's not already taken by another company) and you should probably expect to pay around $10 a year for it. If you can, it's better to get the .com version of your business name, as it's the most common and easiest for customers to remember.

Next, you'll need a hosting account to host your website. The most popular of the larger companies are places like hostgator.com, bluehost.com, 1and1.com, and godaddy.com. I'm not affiliated with any of these sites (although I do personally use some of them) so it's up to you to research them all and choose which one suits your needs and budget best. Expect to pay around $10 a month for hosting your website.

Once you have your domain name and hosting, you can get started. You can either choose to put a blogging platform like Wordpress on your website (recommended) or, if you know how to build static websites using html, you could build your own site. Either way makes no difference to the amount of money you can make.

Use your hosting account's 'help' pages to find out how to install Wordpress on your site (it's usually a one-click process from your control panel in your member's area). Then, once you've got your Wordpress blog set up and installed correctly, you can get blogging.

WHAT DO YOU WRITE ABOUT?

I could tell you to again write information articles and product review-type articles, and those can work, but to really make money, you need to find your 'thing'.

I believe everyone has a 'thing' that is capable of making money online.

For me, it's writing. I found a way to turn my writing into making money by writing about what I know - which is writing predominately about money subjects, since it's a passion of mine to help people take control of their finances. (Although I have written about many other things that are close to my heart, including fertility issues; generally, these were not for financial gain.)

Writing about the things that I am most passionate about and believe in are the ones that earn me the most money online.

So, what is your thing? Are you a singer? Do you think teaching children to read at a young age is important? Do you have experience in dealing with a loved one's mental illness, perhaps?

Most of these can be turned into a profitable business idea, whether that's by selling related products, putting advertising on your site, teaching someone how to do something for a fee, or even writing books like I do.

I'm not telling you to be sleazy about it, nor do I want anyone to take advantage of someone else's situation. But, if you have something worthy to contribute, and believe you have something to say on the matter (and that people would listen and learn from you) then it's one of the most worthwhile and fulfilling ways to make money online.

Starting a Business Offline

Of course, not all good businesses are online; there are hundreds of wonderful businesses that you can start offline in the real world, which have the potential to make you good money.

It could be something as simple as mowing lawns for $30 a pop, or as serious as designing and creating a new product from stay at home mothers designing baby slings and breastfeeding tops, to young guys designing beer bottle cap remover belt buckles.

If they can do it, you can, too! So keep your eyes open, look for opportunities around you, and use your talents.

Earning extra money will definitely help you save up and get out of debt faster. Plus, it might give you are whole new career path, as well. Who knows?

SIX

CHAPTER

6

What to do with the Savings You've Made

B y now, you will be coming to the end of your thirty-day spending detox, and you are probably wondering where to go from here.

While I'll be covering what you should do once you finish in the next chapter, I thought I'd quickly go over some of your options about what you can do with the money that you've saved this month.

The amount that you will have saved will vary from person to person depending on what your lifestyle and income was before you started the challenge. For the average person, it's not uncommon to save a good $500 or more this month.

While $500 might not seem like much, it's a lot richer

than you were just 30 days ago.

If you hadn't done the challenge, you'd have spent it on some random things and might not even have realized where it went. If you can achieve that in such a short space of time, imagine what you could do over a longer period of time.

But let's just focus on the here and now, and not get ahead of ourselves. Let's say that you actually did save $500 (for ease of argument, and for my poor math skills) over this month. What are you going to do with it?

Obviously, that will come down to why you wanted to do the challenge in the first place. It might have been to pay off some debt, save up for something special, or just curb your out-of-control spending habits.

Let's look at these options one by one.

DEBT

According to Wikipedia, the median credit card debt in America is $3,000 with most people owning at least two cards.

So, again, for ease of argument, let's say that you DO

owe exactly $3,000 in credit card debt and you want to pay it off.

Right now, your minimum amount that you have to pay on that balance would be approximately 2.5% p.a., or $10 (whichever is the higher of the two).

And, with an average interest rate of 16% p.a., if you JUST paid the minimum balance every month (at 2.5% of the current balance) it'd end up taking 19 years and 2 months to pay off in full, and you'd be paying an extra $3,147 in interest to the bank during that time.

Nope, that wasn't a typo. Shocking, isn't it? 19 years! Yikes! No wonder debt has such a bad rap.

Now, of course, I realize that most people pay down much more than just the minimum amount required (as they should) but it still shows just how hard it is to get rid of any borrowed money once you start accumulating it.

If you put that one-time payment of $500 on your credit card, and STILL just continued to make the minimum payments, now it'd take you 17 years and 10 months, and you'd pay $2,575 in interest.

So, just by putting that extra on your card upfront,

you've just saved yourself 1 year and 2 months, and an extra $572 interest. Not bad for a little sacrifice, is it?

If you wanted to get rid of it altogether, then all you'd have to do is another four or five 30-day spending detox's (or at least cut back your spending) in the future.

If you have more than one credit card, you might be wondering which one to tackle first.

Generally, most financial planners will tell you to pay off the credit card with the highest interest rate first, and then, when that one is paid off, you can move to the second highest one, and so forth.

The strategy is that you pay the highest amount that you can on the card or debt with the highest rate, and the minimum balance on the others, and keep moving on down as each one gets paid off.

And, while that seems to be the most logical strategy, since you want to get rid of the 'baddest' debt first, I have a slightly different approach that works better with most people.

Pay off the cards that have the lowest balance left on them first, and then move onto the one with the next lowest balance, and so on. I got the idea from Dave

Ramsey (author) and love it. He calls it the Debt Snowball Method.

The reason I like this approach is that you can feel like you are accomplishing something and getting ahead every time you pay off a card.

The smaller the balance left on it, the easier it becomes to pay it off in full. And nothing makes you feel less stressed than having fewer cards to worry about.

Sure, you might end up paying a tiny bit of extra interest in the long run because you haven't chosen the card with the highest interest rate, but that cost is usually negligible compared to the feeling you get when you completely wipe out one of your debts.

It gives you a psychological advantage.

SAVINGS

If you've paid off your credit card or other unsecured debt's, and want to save that money, instead, then you'll be pleased to know that $500 can help make you a millionaire in the right bank account.

It's true.

The only catch is that you'll need to leave it to gain interest for 153 years. Then, without adding another cent, you'll have a cool million (based on a savings account with a compound interest rate of 5%).

What? You don't have 153 years to wait? Hmm... then it looks like you are going to have to save some more money.

Okay then, let's say that every year from now on, you did another spending detox and were able to add another $500 to your original amount. Then, to get to $1 million, it would now take 92 years.

What, that's still a little too long to wait?

Okay, then it looks like you are going to need to add a bit more money to your funds if you want to save $1 million in a much shorter time frame.

So, let's get back to basics.

Where do you Put the Money that you are Saving?

Your regular everyday bank account might seem the best place to put it, but if you use that account for everyday purposes, then pretty soon, that money is going to get used for something else rather than whatever you are saving for.

So, the first step is to set up a separate savings account to put the money into (if you don't have one already).

Looking around at different high interest accounts, you'll find that the majority of the ones offering the best interest rates are those online accounts that you get with Ally Bank and ING Direct. You might find that your bank also offers high interest rates, so it's worth looking at these to see if you want to stay with your own bank for ease of use.

It used to be that it was quite easy to find annual interest rates as high as 5% and 6% p.a. in the U.S., but these days, you are probably looking at under 2%, which means you won't be able to use compound interest to your benefit as much as you used to.

Fortunately, here in Australia, we can still get around 5% in our savings accounts. (* note this was in 2011, we don't get that anymore.)

But don't feel envious: we have 7% to 8% home loans (again this was in 2011), whereas U.S. citizens get a low 3% mortgage. Much nicer!

Whatever interest rate you are able to get, even the small amounts are better than nothing at all. And most people like that bank accounts are much safer than other investments, which promise higher returns.

Okay, so you've got your savings account set up and you've put your $500 in it.

Hopefully during your 30-day spending detox, you realized that much of your spending has been unnecessary, and you want to continue to build your savings by cutting back.

You, hypothetically, can now save an extra $200 a month pretty comfortably, and you will put your tax refund in the account, as well (which, for this hypothetical example, might be another $300). So, you are essentially able to add another $2700 a year to your savings account.

Let's imagine your goal is to save $50,000 for a deposit on a house. You've now got $500, so you still need $49,500 more. By putting away $2700 a year with an interest rate of 1.0%, it will take you 17 years to save up $50,000.

Sounds like a long time, but saving up for 17 years sounds a lot better than paying off the $3,000 credit card that I used in the example earlier. I know what I'd rather be doing in that time.

Remember that time passes whether you are saving money, or not, so at least you'll have something at the end of that time to look forward to.

It's also very possible that you will be able to save up a lot more money than I've used here, especially if you use some of the tips from the last chapter and found some ways of earning extra cash.

But, if savings accounts seem a little slow to build up your money, then there is always investing.

Investing

Investing your money usually scares the bejesus out of most people, but it doesn't have to be as risky as some make out, and can actually help you get further ahead (as long as you choose wisely, that is).

There are many different ways that you can invest your money, including mutual funds, property, stocks, and in businesses (whether directly, or as a venture capitalist).

But let's go over some of the simpler investing methods

to see if any of them are right for you, and go over the pros and cons of each.

Mutual Funds

Mutual funds (or managed funds) are probably the most common way to invest your money. They work by pooling lots of people's money together to invest in property, stocks, bonds, other securities, or a combination of them all - although the majority of most mutual funds do invest in stocks.

It's an easy way for people to get involved in the stock market without having a large amount of capital, because you can invest with as little as $500 and potentially own a small piece of hundreds of different companies.

But, like stocks, there's no guarantee that mutual funds will make money for you. When the markets are going great, then it usually follows that the funds will, as well, but even really great fund managers will not be able to stop the investment from losing money in a down market.

But, if you believe, like I do, that the stock market moves

in cycles, and that after every market crash or recession, there comes a strong period of recovery, just like it has always done throughout history, then it's simply a matter of having faith and waiting for the economic recovery, however long it might take.

Pros:

There are two reasons why I think mutual funds make a good investment, and that includes one: you don't need to know anything about the stock market, and can leave it up to the professional fund managers, and two: you get much higher levels of diversification than you would buying stocks individually. And, diversification lowers risk, which may make it more attractive to some.

Cons:

The cons to investing in mutual funds are that you have no control over what companies the fund invests in, which, if you have control issues like I do, can cause some frustration.

Most mutual funds usually have three different fees: an entry fee, an exit fee, and an annual fee, which can eat into investor's capital.

And, lastly, diversification. Yes, I know I already

mentioned this in pros, but you can be over diversified to the point that you actually minimize your returns and never do better than average in the market.

Stocks

Investing directly in stocks is not for everyone, and you probably will need more money that just $500 to get started (I usually recommend $3,000). However, if the current economic situation hasn't scared you silly, then looking long term at stocks isn't such a bad option.

This isn't a short term solution, though, and if you think you are going to need your savings within five years, then it's not for you.

But, if you have time on your side, then it might be worth looking into, since, historically, stocks have returned an average of 10% p.a., or more, even including especially good and bad years.

The market is cyclical: it usually has a boom period, a slowing of the economy, a crash, a recession, a recovery, another boom period, and so on. That should mean that an economic recovery is due within the next few years (or at least I have my fingers crossed for it to be so; right now the stock market sucks, but I still have faith).

However, there is another way that people invest in stocks, which doesn't take into account of market ups and downs, and that is investing for the income, or dividend yield.

Many companies pay a reasonable dividend to shareholders, which are much higher than standard bank accounts, often as high as 7% or 8% p.a. I bet you wouldn't be as concerned with what the stock price is doing if you were getting dividend checks with that sort of yield on them, would you?

If you are interested in investing for income, then I would still advise that you look at companies with strong fundamentals. There are plenty of good companies listed in the Dow Jones Industrial Average that have good stable financials, and also include high dividend yields of around 5% p.a.

Pros:

You get to own a piece of a company and be a real shareholder (I still get a thrill out of this). If you invest wisely, you can make a good return on your money; at least a lot higher than any bank account can give you. It's fun, too (or at least it is for me).

You can choose to invest just for income so you don't have to worry about stock price ups and downs.

Cons:

You can lose money during market crashes and bear markets. It can be complicated learning how to choose good companies to invest in if you have never done it before, and it can be stressful watching the market move up and down.

BONDS/FIXED Interest Securities

Most people believe bonds to be a safe investment, and, while they ARE much safer than stocks, there is still some risk to be had. But if you understand those risks, then investing in bonds (and I'm talking actual bonds here, not bond funds) then it could be a good option.

The con, of course, is that your money is locked away for a set period of time, say 1 year, 2 years, or 3 years (or whatever time frame of the bond you've chosen has) and you can't touch your money until the maturation date.

On the plus side, the yield, or interest rate, on bonds is usually higher than a regular savings account, so you should be able to make more from them.

If you are going to invest in bonds, then make sure to look for good quality bonds, either corporate, municipal, or treasury, that have a maturation date (don't buy any bonds that don't have this end date) and that you know the yield up front (fixed yields are better for shorter term bonds).

If you can't find good bonds which have yields that are much higher than a savings account, then I'd personally recommend you keep your money in a savings account, because at least you'll be able to access it at a moment's notice.

Pros

Bonds are relatively safe.

Cons

Your money is locked away for lengthy periods, during which you can't touch it. Often, yields are not much higher than you'd get with a regular savings account.

PROPERTY

Property can make a great investment if you have the funds, but since I'm not an expert on investing in property, and you probably won't have enough to get started with just $500, then I would say it's probably not worth delving into here.

But, if you are a property mogul, then let us know about your book, I'd love to read it.

So to Summarize, what SHOULD you be Doing with your Hard Earned Savings?

Step 1.

Obviously, the first step to getting ahead financially is to pay off all your debt first. Before you start saving, or even think about investing, you should try and clear any unsecured debt (credit cards, store cards, personal loans, car loans, etc.). Debt will make you poorer than anything else.

Some of you might have only a little bit of debt, and others will have a lot. Don't feel overwhelmed; just take it a day at a time. If you can last a month without spending, then you'll see that you can cut back, and that you don't need everything you think you do.

I just showed you how just having $3,000 on your credit card would take you nearly 20 years to pay off if you just paid the minimum balance. That's just crazy, and is no way to live.

Your first goal should be trying to get rid of it as fast as you can.

Step 2.

Once you've gotten rid of the unsecured debt, then you can start your emergency fund. Try and save about $2,000 for this, since that is considered the amount most people need every year for unnecessary expenses, and then every time you have to use some of the money, save more to replace it again.

Open up a savings account that is just for this purpose so that it doesn't get mixed up with your everyday account.

Step 3.

Start a *'wish'* savings account. Dream about something you really want to do, and start saving for it. Life is only fun when dreams come true.

You want to save for those special moments and experiences and the things that you REALLY want, and not just think about what you want.

This will probably take most of your time, but knowing that each week, month, or year, you're getting closer to your goal, everything will be worthwhile.

Step 4.

Think about whether you want to invest your money to further your wealth. Yes, there are risks, and it isn't for everyone (and it's okay if it isn't for you) but it can substantially boost your income if you are savvy and have done your homework.

I like the share market, but you might like buying old houses and doing them up, or perhaps you want to invest in safer bonds?

Only do what you feel comfortable with.

Step 5.

Try not to stress about anything. It's not who has the most stuff that wins, in the end. Remember health, family, and friends are still the most important things in your life. Not your stuff.

SEVEN

After the 30 Day Spending Detox

D on't focus on what you are giving up, instead focus on what you are gaining - freedom from debt, financial control, and more time.

You've made it to the end of the 30-day spending detox. **Congratulations**!

Hopefully you got through the whole month without spending any extra money. Even if you had a few small slip-ups, it's still an awesome achievement to have accomplished!

But, you may be wondering what you do now that it's over. Do you go back to your regular spending habits, or has the challenge opened your eyes to not consuming so much?

Generally, most people fall into one of three camps:

- Itching to get let loose in the mall and spend some money again.

- Happy to continue to spend less (or not at all) in the future, and have no desire to fill your house with more stuff. (Down with consumerism.)

- Or, you might be in the middle, which is probably most likely. You have a few things that you delayed buying until now, but, overall, you didn't miss spending that much at all, which makes you think about all the impulse purchases that you've made in the past, which you could easily have lived without.

Whichever camp you fall into, it should have helped you think more mindfully about what you spend your money on, whether you are ready to spend again, or not.

I know when I did it, there were a handful of things that I still needed, and as soon as the month was up, I went out and purchased them.

However, there were also many things that I probably would have purchased, but, after waiting, the desire for them had passed, and I no longer wanted them.

I actually found the challenge much easier than I

thought it would be, and, even though there was plenty that I did buy once the month was over, it was still much less than I would have normally spent if I was not doing the challenge at all.

If you are in the camp that just wants to get back to spending, I would caution you to not let all the good habits that you formed this month go to waste by going on a spending binge to make up for going without.

That doesn't mean that you need to hold off on those items that you really do need, though. In fact, it should actually make you more confident that these items are important, and that you do need them.

Keen For Another Spending Detox?

Think you can handle doing another spending detox to help you to save up even more money? It's not a bad idea if you found this one easy enough.

I've heard of people who have gone a whole year without spending (and you thought one month was extreme!). I'm not sure if I could do a whole year, but I think I could easily do one month on, one month off (except for December, when I couldn't possibly not spend any money).

Whether you choose to do another full month, or perhaps even the odd week or two, whenever you decide to do another one, you'll find it a lot easier, since you know what to expect.

If you have a big debt to pay off, or you are trying to save up for something big, then it could give you a big boost and get you to your goal a lot faster.

Of course, you don't need to do another detox if you think one was enough to get your budget back on track. Often, just one month is enough to keep you mindful of any excess spending that you do.

It's all about control, after all.

And if you choose to either spend or not spend whenever you like, you know that it's possible to live just fine without buying in the short term. And having that control is the real key to becoming financially free.

"I really enjoyed the month, and, while I still do spend occasionally, I've found that I don't want to keep buying things only to throw them out in the future. I've moved house a few times, and every time I move, I hate how many things I have to pack and unpack each time. It's enough to make me want to throw everything out and become a minimalist!" Pat.

If you did enjoy the experience and now realize how much society is a slave to consumerism, you might even think about going minimalist.

Since I started de-cluttering during my spending detox, I have been toying with the idea of paring down dramatically and only living with the bare essentials. Not because I want to go without, but because I want to live with more space and peace. I find having less around me allows me to think more clearly, which, as a writer, helps immensely.

Becoming a minimalist isn't for everyone, but knowing that it's entirely possible to have a different viewpoint on how you live your life can be hugely freeing when all you've been told by marketing is that you need more stuff to be happy.

Happiness does not come from more possessions, and, in fact, I would argue that it just causes more stress, because you have more to clean, house, store, and worry about getting broken or being stolen.

As our world goes more digital, it becomes much easier to live with less things, as now books and photographs can be stored in digital format, news is easier to digest online than reading a newspaper, and even cooking apps and videos are becoming more popular than cookbooks. Imagine a kitchen without a whole shelf of cookbooks cluttering it up and gathering dust because you rarely use them.

Still, I can't really see my family embracing the idea of having a minimalist house, but I can probably persuade them to pare down. Or, at least, that's my aim over the next year or two.

There are many great websites and books dedicated to going minimalist, such as missminimalist.com, and zenhabits.net. If this is something you want to pursue, then I encourage you to check them out.

The Simple Rules Budget

Stopping spending altogether is one thing, but it isn't sustainable for the long term. Having a plan or budget to continue saving and paying off debt is a must going forward.

Now that the month is over and things are getting back to normal, it's probably a good idea to have a look over your budget so that you can keep track of your spending properly, without having to worry about where the money is going again.

Did you have a budget prior to the spending detox? Did you know how much money you were spending each month?

I'm sure you had some idea, but if you are like most people, there are always those days when money just seems to disappear. And, of course, budgets are not just about allocating every penny that you earn, they are also about allocating money to savings and investment goals.

So few people save money these days, and I believe that one of the reasons they don't is that they don't know where to start, or how much they should be putting away.

The usual way that many people save money is, as soon as they get their wages, they pay the bills first, do their usual spending, and whatever is left over at the end of the pay period is put into savings.

Now, if you are savvy enough to know your spending limits, this can work, but if you are like most of us, then you know that there is rarely ever any left over.

So, let's just flip around the order so you do have money to save or pay off debt each pay day.

Now, you've all heard the concept of pay yourself first,

which is where you put money away for yourself before you start paying bills, or buying things, and here's how it works:

As soon as you get your pay, you take out 10% or more (whatever you feel you can comfortable put away without it impacting your other expenses, although 10% should be the minimum) and put it into your savings account or straight into the credit card debt if you still have money owing on that.

The rest of the money goes to paying off the bills, and THEN, whatever is left over is your spending money to spend on whatever you like.

The reason it works is because if you put that money away first, you are less likely to miss it. And, once you get your spending money (last) you won't feel guilty about buying whatever you like, because you'll know that you've already put away your savings and paid your bills.

It also doesn't require that you have to write down every little thing that you purchase, because it doesn't matter what you spend your money on.

Of course, if you find it too easy, then you could probably put up the amount that you put away on savings to a higher percentage and see how you go.

It's about finding that balance about becoming debt free and still having a little fun.

Budgeting for Large Purchases

There may be times that some of things that you want to buy don't fit into your 'spending allowance', as they are larger, or more expensive than your usual everyday spending.

The best way to deal with them is to include them in your savings plan. If you still owe money on credit cards, but you still want the expensive item, then you could do a 50/50 split to save up for it.

So, instead of putting 10% on your credit card, you'd put 5% on it, and use the other 5% to save up for the item. It may take you a little longer, but that time could actually work to your benefit.

While you are saving for it, (and nothing helps boost your savings like a real desire - it makes you stop spending on all the little stuff), you'll have the time to research it, see if there are better alternatives, and will also give you more time to find the best deals and not be tempted by a pushy salesperson who wants you to buy it there and then.

But, what if you need a certain item by a certain day, and you can't delay too long or you'll miss out altogether? Well, short of beg, borrowing, or stealing (which I've already mentioned is not a good option) it means that you are going to have to ramp up your saving and cut back your spending quite a lot.

You already know how to do this, though. You've just learned how. Just rinse and repeat everything you've learned about saving and earning more money.

You'll get there.

SPENDING LESS in the Future

Now that you've got through the month and you know that you can easily spend nothing at all, you have probably realized that there are lots of other ways to cut down your spending, now that you are back to 'normal'.

Have a think about your lifestyle and what you do and don't use on a regular basis.

It may be that you barely use some of the channels on your cable subscription, and you can save a few dollars or more a month by downgrading. Or that you can get a better phone plan, or even just reduce the amount of calls or texts that you make.

For example, it might be worth getting a Skype account for free video calls, or use Twitter for text messaging if your carrier doesn't give you free text messages.

If you think about things, there are probably lots of ways that you can save a few cents here and there and all of those little savings will add up over time to a big sum.

The key to cutting back successfully is to find out ways of either dropping the things that you don't enjoy that you currently pay for, or by substituting something cheaper in their place.

With real diets, often the people that are most successful are those that substitute one high fat food for a lower calorie, healthier alternative, and you can do the same with your spending diet, as well, by finding alternatives to all your favorite expenses.

This can be fun as you make a game of finding things that give you just as much pleasure, but are cheaper. It could also be that you explore new things that you had never thought about, and you just might find something that you love that you may not have tried before.

"I never really had time to take photographs before, except for the odd photo of my friends here and there" said Daniel, *"but during this month, I took my camera as I walked around our suburb, taking pictures of buildings, interesting plants and trees, and other interesting objects. I realized that I have a real passion for photography now, and want to start a blog with the pictures I've taken."*

Perhaps you enjoy reading your favorite magazine online for free, instead of buying a subscription (I know I personally subscribe to all my mags on the iPad now, which is a lot less expensive, and creates far less clutter than it used to).

If you are a bit of a bookworm, then you can get most books now in the eBook version for your Kindle, iPad, or Nook, which works out much cheaper than buying paperback editions.

Amazon even has a Kindle Daily Deals promotion that it runs that dramatically cuts the cost of an eBook a day by around 70% or more. I've even seen popular $9.99 eBooks cut to just 0.99 cents with this promo.

The digital world that we now live in actually makes things a lot cheaper than they used to be. By going onto iTunes, you can purchase one song, instead of having to buy a whole CD, and news is delivered for free on most websites so you no longer need a newspaper subscription.

IT'S NOT ALL **About Spending Though**

This challenge wasn't just about gaining perspective and control over your spending and saving money, but also about living simpler with less stress.

By not shopping as much this month, you would have had more time to spend with your family, or simply do nothing at all. With everyone rushing to get everything done these days - from work, to family, to activities - nobody really takes the time to just sit and be in the moment.

Just spending a few quiet moments without distractions can be a wonderful stress reliever, especially if you now feel like you have real control over your finances, again.

What Are You Going To Do, Now That The Month Is Over?

Now is a good time to reflect on the past thirty days to see what you found easy and what you found difficult.

You might have surprised yourself and realized that not spending was a lot easier than you thought, or you might be itching to get back to normal again.

Make a list of all those things that you won't be giving up altogether.

It might be that you can't take a packed lunch to work every day, because it was too difficult, so you are going back to buying your lunch again. And if that's the case, don't feel guilty about it, but perhaps you can find alternative or cheaper food options. It could be that you could buy cans of soda from the grocery store at a discount price and take one to work, yet still purchase your sandwich everyday so that you don't have to make it.

Or, maybe you liked having your morning coffee at home, because it gave you a few extra minutes to sit down before you rushed for work, but you still buy one on the way home.

Introduce some little extras back into your life to keep it fun, but don't go overboard. We all know that people who are on too restrictive a diet will binge periodically, and you don't want this to happen to your great spending patterns, so allowing yourself little luxuries here and there (as long as you have budgeted for them and can afford it) will keep you sane and not have you feel like you are denying yourself.

In Summary

Now that you've finished your 30-day spending detox, it is a great time to evaluate yourself and your spending habits to see what you can and can't continue with.

While you probably found it sometimes difficult and other times easy, overall, it should have given you a really good perspective on your wants and desires, versus your real needs.

It should also have given you a chance to ask yourself why you want the things that you do. Is it because it would make your life better, or because you were swayed by the marketing messages behind the product?

I know for me, personally, it was a huge eye opener, because often, I never really want the product, but rather the feelings and benefits that the product promises.

Intellectually, I know it's probably just hype, but that doesn't stop the desire. So, by interrupting this pattern, I could see that after the initial 'I want' wore off (usually a few days) I no longer wanted the item, at all.

For me, breaking that initial impulse buy was a strong key to taking back control of my spending habits. It hasn't made me stop spending altogether, but has curbed a lot of the things I really don't need when I have a perfectly functioning item at home that will do the job just as well. So, by fixing my thinking, I've fixed my spending, as well.

It's now up to you to move forward with a strong plan that is sustainable for your lifestyle, but that doesn't cause further spending or debt problems. And, if you learned something during this month, then I hope that you found the experience worthwhile.

Afterword

Phew, you made it! You went a whole month without spending. Yes, a whole MONTH! Good for you!

So, what did you learn?

For me, apart from learning about myself and my attitudes toward money, I also found that people thought that I was crazy for even considering not buying things.

Everyone I told that I was doing it said that they couldn't possibly go without spending for a whole month. When I was tweeting about some of my experiences, one person re-tweeted my tweet with some question marks at the end, implying it was a very strange thing to want to do.

My own mother, who probably needs to do a few no-spend months, herself, just nodded her head and tut-tutted, as if it's just another one of my crazy schemes again.

Many people think it's a crazy thing to do because it's so extreme. Shopping is so ingrained in our culture that to not do it regularly is like shunning society. And I love society. I just don't like being in debt.

Especially when we, and by that, I mean *me*, should know better. And especially when you can't find your babies' chest rub in the middle of the night, because you have too much stuff.

Enough already. Slow down. Relax. Gain control. Stop the out of control spending.

Not forever. Just for thirty little teeny tiny days.

But you know this already, because you came on this journey yourself. I promised you that you'd save money. I sincerely hope that you did. I promised that you'd gain a new perspective on how you spend your money. I have no doubt that you did. And I promised you control back over your finances, which you already had. You just needed to believe it.

Thank you for joining me. Thank you for reading my book. And thank you for believing.

Tracey

APPENDIX

A

My Own 30 Day Spending Detox Journal

When I was doing my spending detox, I decided to write down how I was feeling or little observations that I made during the day.

Sometimes they were serious and thoughtful, and other times I wrote something to make myself laugh and make the process fun.

While I never actually intended to publish this in the beginning, after I had finished this book, I thought I'd include my notes here, in case you were interested in reading it, as I thought it might make someone laugh (either at me, or with me).

DAY 1

Didn't spend a cent today. This is easy. No problem.

DAY 2

I really need a haircut. My hair looks awful, and it's sticking out at all angles. I should have got it cut before I started this challenge.

So, my options are either to wait, or cut it myself. Since I'm not going to cut it myself – too many childhood memories of crooked fringes – that means I'm going to have to wait it out. Bobby pins will be my friend this month. And hats.

DAY 3

Husband went to see the movie Transformers today. I told him that I thought we weren't going to spend any money this month. He told me that he thought that I was not going to spend any money this month, not him.

DAY 4

I needed to go grocery shopping today, and since my local grocery store is located inside a mall, I decided to have a quick look inside one of the department stores before I got our food.

While I knew I couldn't spend any money in the store, I told myself that I was just there to browse and see what they had. I saw a few tops that I wanted to try on, and a pair of shoes on sale. And, while I didn't purchase any of them, I started thinking about when I would come back and get them once this challenge was over.

It was then that I started to remember why I was even doing this challenge to begin with, not spend money, and here I was, planning on trying to get around the rules by shopping in my head and delaying any purchases for the following month.

This sucks.

DAY 5

My friend had a baby today. I didn't pre-purchase a gift. That means I need to wait another 25 days before I go and see her and the new addition to her family. I said congrats on Facebook, though - that counts, right?

DAY 6

I find weekends the easiest times to be on a spending detox. That is, as long as I remember to stay away from the shopping malls.

De-cluttering the house is actually making things a lot easier, though, because it sucks, and now I'm thinking I don't want more stuff to put back in the nice neat spaces that I'm making. So far, I've removed the two bookshelves that were on either side of the fireplace (they were ugly) and got boxed up about 70% of the books to either give away, or donate to charity.

Mister Five had gotten into the spirit, too, by putting all the toys that he no longer plays with into a box to give away. Baby Girl took a few things out, though, and squirreled them away in her room somewhere.

Will get to that later, though. Right now the living area is number one priority.

Although clearing the bookcases away did reveal a different color on the wall, which means I need to repaint, I want to paint, anyway, as the previous owner thought a pale dirty green color would be a good choice.

But *paint does cost money, so I'll have to live with the two toned walls for another few weeks. (Or perhaps longer; I still don't want to spend unnecessary money and may continue the no-spending after the challenge is over.)*

DAY 7

It's now been one full week that I've been on the spending detox. So far, it hasn't been that difficult, but then most diets that I've done have always been relatively easy in the first week, as well. It isn't until the 2nd or 3rd week that things started to get more difficult.

The only thing that is different between now and when I started the challenge is how much more serious I feel that the credit card debt has become.

I'm not sure that's because I'm finally coming to full realization about it, or because last night Husband did an audit on our biggest credit card over the past four months, and I could see, right there in an excel spreadsheet, exactly where our money is going.

I read somewhere recently that the average four person household spends $382 a week on food. We are spending around $500 a week. $500 a week – what are we buying?

Now that's a combination of both take-away and grocery food, but still – that seems very high.

I've also started looking at a few frugality and cheapskate websites for tips on how to reduce the household bills.

They have tips like how to make your own laundry powder. Am I really at the stage where I have to make my own laundry powder? Bank Balance: "Yes, Tracey."

I'm not sure how I feel about that.

Denial?

DAY 8

I had a bit of a panic attack last night. I couldn't think straight, and, while I know that compared to some people, our debt situation is not that huge, it was freaking me out that I had this credit card bill looming over me with no real income coming in. Scared how we are going to pay it.

DAY 9

Went food shopping today and was happy to get my groceries down to about $120 for four days worth of meals. That's impressive for me. There were a lot of items on special, and lots of generic brands, so I was very impressed with myself. I couldn't, however, bring myself to buy cheaper nappies [diapers] and stuck with the most expensive brand. I've tried cheaper nappies before, and they leaked everywhere, so I'm not willing to take the risk again.

I'll also need to learn how to be a better cook. I got a packet of chocolate cake mix that was half price, but it didn't include icing in the pack, so I purchased a separate chocolate icing kit. I realise that chocolate icing is probably terribly easy (I would imagine it is some combination of icing sugar [confectioner's sugar], cocoa, milk, and butter) but since I've never made it, I wasn't going to risk it.

Obviously, being a good cook will help in making inexpensive meals. That will come in time.

I'm actually finding the challenge far easier than I imagined I would. Sure, there are a few things that I've earmarked to get next month, but I've had time to think about whether I really need them, or if they're an impulse buy. The only things that I'm buying next month are things I really need. Plus, this extra time is allowing me to see where I can get the best deals when it's actually time to hand over the cash.

It's been rather cold here in the past few days. Winter and summer are naturally more expensive when it comes to heating and cooling. I've had the heating on now all day so far, which is going to make an expensive utility bill when it comes.

I've been looking into different ways to save heating costs, and most of them include things like heavier curtains to keep the warmth inside, sealing up door cracks, and window seals. Adding extra layers of clothes.

The only one I can really do right now is to add layers. I've been wearing my dressing gown around the house over my clothes. I must look awesome. But at least I'm warm. Obviously, you can't think about looking your best when you are in financial survival mode.

DAY 10

Really need to cut my hair. It's still sticking out at weird angles, and a bit at the front is longer than the rest, and it looks odd. Not sure I can get away from calling it 'trendy'.

DAY 11

Cut my own hair. Well, not all of it - but that piece of the front that was longer than the rest and sticking out. Turned out well, and looks good - feel like I can live with my hair for a few more weeks. This has given me confidence that I will be able to trim my own hair more often. Might be a false confidence. Not sure I'll risk it again. Or maybe I will... mwahahaha. Have no idea who I'm doing the false evil laugh for. Doesn't even make sense. Yes, boredom is setting in with no shopping to do.

DAY 14

Baby girl needs new singlets [vests/tank tops, depending on what you call them - you know, undergarment little tops that keep you warm - those] as she has nearly outgrown her current ones. But I can't just go and buy them, because I'm not spending this month. But should I? Is this 'experiment' of mine really fair on those who didn't choose to take part? Am I denying her clothing that she needs because I'm too stubborn to not spend for another two weeks?

Is this really about new singlets? Why am I still calling it an 'experiment' when I still have massive credit card debt? Am I still in denial?

DAY 15

Needed to buy some new services to help one of my websites. Is it really a need? Yes, it will help my business. But is it a necessity? How do you judge whether paying for a service is a need or a want? It's not like I saw it in a shop window and drooled over it, it's merely something I think will benefit my online business.

Does not spending even have to apply to business?

Even though my business is 'me' as a writer - should that be separate as 'me' as a mother and housewife? Does it even apply?

Too confusing. Will wait until next month and re-evaluate whether it's important to grow the biz or not.

After all, it's not as if I'm wasting money on something that will hide away in my closet collecting dust - it's something that could potentially help me earn more in my business.

But I'll still wait. Maybe this waiting will help me grow.

DAY 16

I can't remember today. Did it happen?

DAY 17

Read an article in a women's mag about an amazing new light therapy thing that helps make you look younger. Starting to really want it. False hope, why do you tempt me so?

DAY 18

Credit card is looking better. Still not zero, yet, but not keeping me awake at night, either. The kids DO still keep me awake at night - when do mothers get a full night's sleep again?

DAY 19

I mentioned something on Twitter about not spending, using the hash tag #nospendmonth. Someone re-tweeted my post with some question marks and explanation points, basically to highlight how crazy the tweet was. Is it really that silly?

DAY 20

Oh, god, I've got lots of gray hairs showing. Can't get my hair colored for another week and a half. Will stay indoors and only venture out if I can't help it. Thank goodness its winter and I'm not expected to socialize.

DAY 22

Really wanted to spend money today. This is hard.

DAY 25

Was watching The Block [home renovation reality show] and I so want to get into fixing up this house. Sick of the pale green two-toned walls. Have been checking out home decorating websites online. Everything is tempting me. Perhaps I'll have to ban the TV/iPad/Internet to live without spending. Secluded hut in woods is looking better and better.

DAY 30

Last day. Will be able to spend tomorrow. Not sure how I feel about it. On one hand, I can't wait to go and get my hair done, but, on the other, I like that my credit card is now down to only two thirds of what it was when I started.

Save or spend? Save or spend? Hey, I wonder if this experiment would make a good book?

About the Author

Tracey Edwards is a writer and author.

Her goal is to help others get ahead financially, and also to make budgeting and finance fun (come on, it can be fun, can't it?).

She grew up in country Victoria (Australia) and now lives in sunny Brisbane Australia.

Also by Tracey Edwards

_____

My Other Books

Shopping for Shares: The Everyday Woman's Guide to the Australian Stock Market

ISBN: 978-0-7303-7504-3 (2ND EDITION)

September 2011. Shopping for Shares is the essential girls guide to get you choosing, buying and profiting from the Australian stock market.

$0 to Rich: The Everyday Woman's Guide to Getting Wealthy

ISBN: 978-0-7314-0733-0

January 2008. Written specifically for women, $0 to Rich aims to be a girl's personal financial coach, guiding readers towards achieving their own financial goals by following five easy steps.

Find Me:

traceywritesbooks.com